THE
SHOEBLACK
AND THE
SOVEREIGN

THE
SHOEBLACK
AND THE
SOVEREIGN

REFLECTIONS
ON
▼ ETHICS ▼
AND
FOREIGN POLICY

GEORGE
WALDEN

ST. MARTIN'S PRESS, NEW YORK

Library of Congress Cataloging-in-Publication Data

Walden, George.
    The shoeblack and the sovereign.

    "A Thomas Dunne book."
    1. International relations—Moral and ethical aspects.
2. United States—Foreign relations—1945–
—Moral and ethical aspects.   I. Title.
JX1255.W35 1988 172'.4   88–15853
ISBN 0–312–02281–6

Design by SNAP·HAUS GRAPHICS/DIANE STEVENSON

First Edition
10 9 8 7 6 5 4 3 2 1

Grateful acknowledgments to Professor J.V.W. Quine for looking at the paper this book is based on; to Dr. J.A. Marenbon, Fellow of Trinity College, Cambridge, and Professor Onora O'Neill of Essex University for their advice; and to Dr. Benjamin H. Brown, Director of the Fellows' Program at the Centre for International Affairs of Harvard University.

CONTENTS

INTRODUCTION

This book springs from a period spent at Harvard University several years ago. After nearly twenty years as a diplomat, specializing in Communist affairs and working closely with American friends and colleagues, I thought it a good time and place to reflect on morality and foreign policy. During those years I became acutely aware of Americans' particular sensitivity to the ethical aspect of international relations and was increasingly struck by the relatively sparse attention the subject attracts in Europe. On the American side there are clear historical reasons for this, among them the Puritan tradition and its influence on the U.S. view of the outside world. In Europe, the British see themselves—conveniently enough—as embodying both the moral and the utilitarian aspects of foreign policy, while the French affect to dispense with ethical considerations entirely, and the Germans have evolved from Realpolitik to a prudent pragmatism.

This does not make the Europeans any wickeder, any more than the United States' fixation on what it believes to be good and right internationally, as well as expedient, necessarily makes its actions more virtuous. But these ethical preoccupations do condition the nature, evolution, and presentation of American policy and are at the root of many of the frustrations and misunderstandings within and beyond the Atlantic Alliance. They also have a close bearing on the stability, or otherwise, of the superpower relationship.

I should say at once that I do not subscribe to the view of those Europeans who see the search for ethical policies as a source of weakness in America's international relationships. We would be on firmer critical ground if our own approach to foreign policy, however it is defined, had been a little more successful in Europe than the first ninety years of the century suggest. It would be comforting for Europeans to be able to counterpose their own effortlessly inherited wisdom in these matters—as in others—to the raw, unworldly adhesion to first principles of our American brothers. But a moment's reflection reveals little scope for superior cynicism.

Europeans would do well to remember how much they themselves have benefited from what might be called the idealist strain in American policies, not least in the military rescue of Europe during two World Wars and then in its economic rescue after World War II: These were genuinely moral acts, based on the enlightened defense of the freedom and welfare of others, as well as on the self-interest of the United States. After each conflagration the United States sought to follow through its war effort by promoting a more virtuous international order. President Woodrow Wilson's Fourteen Points did not save Europe's soul, despite the fervor with which he espoused and sought to implement them. But the moral thrust of American policy was by no means spent, and it is often forgotten how much the creation of the European Economic Community after World War II owes to the persistent prompting of U.S. diplomacy. The United States had been preaching the sermon of federalism for some time, and in the post-war period seemed aware of the historical continuities. On August 12, 1947, *The Buffalo Times* wrote in all sincerity, if not entirely to the point: "The peoples in the ruins of Europe can take heart from the perils that beset America in 1787."

Europe was an obvious market for U.S. ethical exports, and there was a strong whiff of moral earnestness behind America's encouragement to the old continent to unite. It was not just a matter of the self-evident economic, political, and military need for Europe to pull together after spending so much wealth and blood tearing itself apart: For the United States European integration was a moral as well as a practical imperative. A federal structure in Europe was seen as *right* as well as necessary—not least because the vision was based on American experience.

The European episode had a happy outcome in the emergence of the European Economic Community. But even when thrusting good advice on friends, Americans tended to overdo things. Such was the strength of their convictions and their determination to carry them through into practice that they deliberately structured the Marshall Plan in such a way as to force the Europeans to cooperate. These methods were not always suited to the removal of the incrustations of centuries of European in-fighting, and the United States was obliged to assume the roles of honest broker, fussing midwife, and blustering paterfamilias to get its moral imperatives across.

With such encouragement, it was a miracle that Europe survived at all, let alone prospered. But it is arguable that without this ethical importuning and the practical assistance of the Marshall Plan, the Common Market (then the Community) would have been pieced together a good deal later, if at all.

By the 1980s the United States' reputation as moral mentor was badly tarnished in European eyes. If a single cause has to be pinpointed, it must be the way the country was seen to have pursued the containment of Communist expansionism. From the Dulles era through Vietnam and to the nuclear tensions of recent years confidence in the United States' ethical leadership has been eroded abroad and subjected to destructive critical analysis at home. To have reached a stage where large sections of the public in Europe and around the world, who are by no means dupes of Moscow, feel justified in making an easy equivalence between the superpowers suggests that there is something badly wrong, both with their perceptions and with the formulation and projection of American policy itself. Those Europeans who act in this way are of course in a sense casting themselves in the role of moralizers. It is easy to slip into such a role when passing judgment on matters concerning the superpowers, since Europeans themselves no longer face the supreme ethical choices that the United States confronts as leader of the Alliance. Moderate habits can come with modest means.

Just as it is impossible to know the United States without admiring the country, so it is easy to sympathize with the fierce indignation of its citizens when they are put on the same moral footing as what is still the world's largest, most sophisticated, and most brutal oppressor of individual liberty and of the human spirit. The fact that the parallel is so frequently made by Europeans who live in the shadow of the Soviet threat, but who cannot yet exert themselves economically to the point of shouldering the full burden of their own defense, does nothing to temper American resentment. The temptation for a renascent United States to retreat from its moral obligation to Europe in response is disturbingly easy to understand.

If the United States, bruised and embittered by European ingratitude and international misunderstanding, were to withdraw into itself and abandon its distinctive style of ethically based foreign policy for a new mode of Realpolitik *à l'européene*, as the country is urged to do from time to time by Europeans, the first victim would be Europe herself. In recent years there has been no lack of American politicians, journalists, and academics to make the point with characteristic American candor.

Faced with this threat, the most prudent reaction would be to mute one's criticism of American policies: The first duty of any practitioner of Realpolitik is surely to keep his peace with his own principal protector. A less prudent—maybe even foolhardy—response would be to join in the reexamination of the first principles of American foreign policy, which has been underway in the United States for some years now, and particularly the whole question of the moral element in its worldview. Yet, for better or worse, this is what this book seeks to do—though the difficulty of integrating ethics into foreign policy is not an American monopoly, and other countries feature too.

For a European, the ethical examination of U.S. foreign policy may seem a hazardous enterprise. The risk of appearing to relapse into European condescension and of adding one's mite to existing misunderstandings is high. Yet it seems clear that Europe, with its own economic, social, and defense problems as well as the unavoidable ambiguities of its foreign policy, is in no position to condescend. It seems equally clear that allies have a duty to say openly what is on their minds: If Anglo-Saxons cannot speak frankly to one another, who can? The need for frank speaking arises from the danger of our foreign policies being dominated by moralistic attitudes. This is by no means a purely American phenomenon: To an extent it is a characteristic Anglo-Saxon affliction. Palmerston was, among other things, a liberal moralist, and Britain is still not averse to an occasional moralistic fit itself.

But the United States' position is unique. I start from the premise that American history, power, and ethical assumptions combine to place the country on a precarious eminence in international relations. Nobody can be blamed for deciding to pitch his policies on the highest available ground, and the world owes a great deal to America's moral mountaineering. But equally, Americans must expect in return to feel a little lonely up there from time to time. Inevitably, those who proclaim high principles are harshly judged when they fall short of their own ideals.

The uniqueness of the United States' position has been highlighted by the recent Soviet-American summits. History will tell us how far they were historic. The advent of the new Soviet leader, Mikhail Gorbachev—assuming it signals a permanent change, which is of course a considerable assumption—and his new approach to international questions in general and to nuclear matters in particular—

also highlight the moral responsibilities of the Soviet Union, which can easily be forgotten as we contemplate our own shortcomings. But that is a subject in itself, which this book does not attempt to encompass. All that needs to be said is that, although Communist societies do not possess the basic prerequisite of a consistently "moral" foreign policy—a functioning democracy—it would be a typical piece of moralism to banish them or other countries with different values or traditions to outer darkness and to assume that such regimes are incapable of moral acts or of self-improvement.

I start from the position that Western democracies, as morally superior societies for all their blemishes, should be more demanding of themselves than we can expect closed or semi-closed societies to be. That is why this book does not seek to draw consolation from the iniquities of alien regimes; rather, it seeks to confront our own dilemmas. This is one of those occasions when the mote in our own eye is more important than the beam in the other fellow's, simply because we can do something about it.

THE
MORALITY
BUSINESS

The windiest militant trash
Important Persons shout
Is not so crude as our wish . . .
—W. H. AUDEN, "September 1,
1939"

▼

What is a truly "moral" foreign policy? The subject
has been endlessly debated, and yet we seem no nearer to
a clear definition. In the sciences, when a *cul de sac* is
reached, the practice is to wonder whether the right questions have been asked and whether research and argument
have been deflected into false, fruitless, or already ex-
hausted fields of enquiry. In the ethics of international affairs there is no lack of material that retreads, refines, or
merely summarizes ground often admirably covered elsewhere. It seems that the time has come to approach the
problem from less familiar angles.

Another, more pressing need is to challenge the growth of attitudes in the study of the subject that have more to do with pseudo-morality than with the genuine article. One of the most disturbing trends in some recent work on foreign policy ethics is the evidence that moralistic assumptions are becoming embedded in the study of morality itself.

In that sense, this book has more to do with moralism than with morality. The descent from the latter to the former is an easy transition, imperceptibly accomplished. Like the degeneration of art into artiness, sentiment into sentimentality, or faith into religiosity, it leads not just to a mere by-product of the original but to a perversion of it. Moralism is not just diluted morality, but its very opposite: The evasion or abandonment of ethical responsibility. The distinction is elusive but crucial, and the reluctance to make it can lead to horribly tangible results in international relations.

One of the twin pillars of morality is practicality—the other being "rightness" itself. When either pillar crumbles, moralism is the result. When it influences the formation of government policy, moralism is dangerous because it leads to decisions that inevitably bring failure and with it the risk of exaggerated counter-reactions. As a consequence, policy will lack stability.

When the new and flourishing study of "practical ethics" fails to provide a disinterested, reflective analysis of problems in the conduct of foreign policy, and becomes instead an instrument for the making of moralistic judgments, the implications are even more profound. Governments need to be constantly called to account by powerful, coherent, and respected voices, and in a sophisticated modern democracy the voice of the intellectual establishment should be among the most pervasive in this running critique. But if the study of morality itself becomes a vehicle for moralism, if—as Thomas Carlyle once said in another context—even the very tailors have become sansculottists, that voice may reverberate more loudly for a moment, but in the end it will rightly be disregarded.

There is nothing like a combination of moralistic government and moralizing critics to bring out the worst in everyone. Finally, all we are left with is a debased form of romanticism, in its sense of extravagance and excess of feeling: A recipe for ultimate failure as the moral vision collides with reality and is destroyed. In foreign policy, as elsewhere, failure brings bitterness and a search for scapegoats or, alternatively, excessive self-recrimination, which can add a new twist to the spiral of escapist psychology in countries, as in people.

Examples are sadly over-familiar. The failure of an attempt to implant or protect democratic virtues by force in an inhospitable climate is followed by an over-dramatized access of self-doubt, insecurity, and vulnerability. This in turn can feed a romantic over-emphasis on the technology of defense, with its Faustian exclusion of the human factor, unnerving allies more than adversaries. Eventually this emphasis too can provoke a lurch back towards more conciliatory policies, which are likely to rebound too far or too suddenly in the other direction. Such fluctuations are invariably accompanied by geyserlike eruptions of public sentiment, pushing each policy far beyond its natural limitations into unwise courses of action or dangerous rhetoric, and producing an inevitable counter-reaction, as each new bout of moralism engenders its opposite.

The result in practical political terms is more or less chronic instability in the sphere of politics—international relations—where stability is most needed. With each new convulsion, new uncertainties grow and with them new fears and suspicions as moral absolutes point in new directions. At one moment the Russians appear as a people with an unexpectedly human face with whom we can do business, by which the world might yet be saved. A year later the same country and people are seeking "windows of opportunity" to launch a nuclear onslaught on the West, necessitating urgent countermeasures that are horribly expensive both in terms of cash and allied cohesion. Then again, under new leadership the adversary seems miraculously transformed: Some good has somehow sprung from an evil system, which appears capable of striving for self-reform in a way not previously thought possible or allowed for in the West's political calculations. Overwhelmed by the discovery that we are dealing with rational human beings, we hasten to conclude agreements with them.

For years, the Chinese present themselves to the moralizer's imagination as a hideous combination of the Red and Yellow perils, stopping at nothing, sweeping across Asia and Africa like an army of ants. A decade later they are a dignified, sober, industrious people with whom business can be done, too—business that does not exclude the sale and purchase of weaponry. At one instant the Third World is peopled with basically sympathetic folk with whom more or less enjoyable suppers can be had with different lengths of spoon. Suddenly again, the whole scene changes, and all are presumed hostile till they declare and demonstrate abiding and exclusive friendship.

The recent "Irangate" affair fits neatly into this disturbing pattern of unpredictability. The morality or otherwise of what was done and the extent of the president's responsibility have naturally preoccupied public attention. But just as disturbing is the sudden switch of status of a country that is at one moment the incarnation of infamy and at the next a secret partner in underhand negotiation.

Clearly, these traumatic reevaluations of more or less permanent international realities are to some extent a function of events—Afghanistan, the Cultural Revolution in China, Iran—and of the changes in government in the Soviet Union or the United States. But they also have a good deal to do with the United States' difficulty in keeping an upright stance on the high pinnacle of morality to which its foreign policy aspires; one step down from that slippery summit and the country is engulfed in a moralistic mire, its foothold on reality gone. Moralism has many drawbacks, but chief amongst them for our purposes is that it leads, inexorably, to inconsistency—by common consent the particular vice of American foreign policy, just as generosity of spirit is its particular virtue. This inconsistency, which worries many Americans of all political persuasions at least as much as it worries some Europeans—and some Russians—is one reason for probing more deeply into some of the sources of moralism in the United States' worldview (and indeed in that of other countries too) and its manifestations in international relationships.

There are other, more fundamental reasons for taking ethics and the distortions that ethical thinking can so easily undergo with a new seriousness. In recent years the pace of foreign policy discussion, formation, and execution seems to have accelerated geometrically, in part because of the effects of the electronic media. More recently still, we have seen the nuclear stakes shorten abruptly—as they did five years ago—then suddenly lengthen again, almost overnight. We may feel comforted for a moment when change seems to point in the direction of a new sanity. But whether as members of the public, as philosophers, or as foreign policy specialists, a certain bewilderment at the sheer speed of these evolutions may modify our rapture. In short, we may feel a sense of moral disorientation.

It would be absurd to lay the blame for the almost spiritual unease this feeling can engender solely at the United States' door, though there have been plenty of attempts to do so, notably in the United States itself. Because of its distinctive traditions and foreign policy attitudes, there is greater sensitivity to and concern about the moral implications of these policy fluctuations on one side of the Atlantic than on the other, as well as a greater demand for explanations.

In the United States few demands are allowed to remain for long unsatisfied. And sure enough, a whole new branch of philosophy has been evolving to meet the need for ethical guidance in foreign affairs, as in other fields of public policy. Whether in biotechnology, abortion, nuclear weapons, or our obligations towards the Third World, the study of "practical ethics" or the "philosophy of public affairs" can only be welcomed. In the case of foreign policy the tradition was of course already there in centuries of largely theological debate over just and unjust wars. Now it has acquired a modern, secular form.

Its more distinguished practitioners have added a sound new dimension to the study of international affairs. Given its particular concern with such matters, it is logical that much of the best work in the field is done in the United States: Stanley Hoffman's *Duties Beyond Borders* and Joseph Nye's *Nuclear Ethics* are just two of the more recent examples. What country other than the United States could boast entire journals devoted to the subject, such as *Ethics and International Affairs,* recently launched by the Carnegie Council for Foreign Relations? I know of no Soviet equivalent.

But this sudden new expansion in practical ethics has highlighted some disturbing weaknesses in the new discipline. As the publications pour out, it is easy to become concerned about some of the directions this work is taking, both because of an unhealthily close identification with certain political attitudes and because of the moral assumptions that underlie these attitudes.

The new philosophy treads a precariously narrow line. On the one hand, it will rightly be judged by the practicality of its theories; on the other, by how far it is concerned with disinterested inquiry and how far with giving intellectual respectability to this or that political party or pressure group. For Aristotle, ethics is a part of politics; judging by some of the early products of the new ethics industry, that is only too clearly the case. But Aristotle meant politics in a more reflective, abstract sense: He certainly did not have in mind the selective underpinning of the views of a particular faction or party on the events of the day by an appeal to the less transient truths of moral philosophy.

The impression is inescapable that as an exercise in practical philosophy, the morality business is simply going too far. In its anxiety to free itself from the cramped cocoon of the traditional study of ethics, it risks becoming relentlessly, embarrassingly contemporaneous—like a respectably aged parent on a spree. It is refreshing and enlightening to have clear minds and logical principles applied to the professional inexactitudes of diplomats and statesmen. These are qualities that are permanently in short supply. But there is no shortage of foreign policy critics, pure and simple. The surface of events is well combed by the press, and the "issues" glossed and glazed by highly qualified commentators. What we do not get enough of and what our new moral philosophers too infrequently give us is any deeper understanding of the underlying ethical mechanisms of public affairs as a whole, and of international affairs in particular.

It is easier to mount a principled assault on—or defense of—American policy in Nicaragua or Vietnam and its consequences than to probe the moral dynamics between government and people or the responsibilities of the media—all of which have a crucial role to play in the formation and execution of these policies. It is more gratifying to deliver oneself of an ethical indictment of the Republican administration's position in Central America than to probe and dissect its ultimate source in the fears, suspicions, misguidedness, nobility of soul, or sheer indifference of the American electorate and to trace the moral conveyor belt through to the White House. In the ethics industry, as in some other walks of life, the impression is that there are too many people gesticulating from the bridge and too few left seeing what is going on in the engine room.

It is sometimes necessary, and always diverting, to make moral judgments on the conduct of governments, and the more moralistic a government's policies appear to be, the greater the temptation to respond in kind. It is far more taxing to explain why we think of relations between states as fundamentally different from those between individuals; whether we are right to expect higher standards from countries than people; and why it is assumed, as it so frequently is, often without argument, that the formation of foreign policy is an ethically inferior aspect of human activity. If it is admitted that a moral continuum exists between states and the people who compose them, from voters to presidents, why is it that all concerned seem so often at pains to minimize it? How are we to account for the yawning dissociation between personal and public moral responsibilities, which the new philosophy has done so little to bridge and a good deal to entrench?

It is certainly not a question of seeking to mute criticism or controversy. There are many areas where it would be good to see moral philosophy take a bold stand. Who else but philosophers, for example, can tell the simple truth to the man in the street of the modern Western democracy that in the formation of public policy, foreign and domestic, he has obligations as well as prerogatives—not only a right to be heard but a duty to understand? There is not much future for politicians or journalists in catechizing the public; even the Church seems increasingly unwilling to do so.

No one wants to inhibit moral philosophers from playing their searchlight more freely across the whole range of public policy. It is simply that it is their job not to illuminate the surface but to penetrate deeper. We need more convincing answers than we have seen so far on the moral status not just of the actors and actions on the foreign policy stage but of those who throng the *coulisses* and the auditoria and of those who indirectly condition the scene of the action: The media and the intellectuals—including philosophers themselves—who exert a growing influence on foreign policy.

We need to know more too about the functions of the new technologies—whether of communication or nuclear destruction—and their weight in the ethical equation. Is it possible that these technologies are of such potency that they inhibit the formation of rational moral choices, promoting instead new varieties of moralism? What more promising area of ethical exploration than the chasm that is opening between the technical sophistication of weaponry, fabricated by man's extraordinary ingenuity, and the infinite simplicities of public opinion, engineered by the equally ingenious electronic media—between the rapid evolution of self-destructive potential and the failure to develop an educated democracy to control it?

Moral philosophy is commonly agreed to be a notoriously difficult and diffuse subject. In the study of the ethics of foreign policy the scope for misunderstanding is especially generous. Already distinctive patterns of confusion are emerging. If these are not checked, the credibility of the new discipline will be undermined before it is securely established.

Put simply, the ethical study of foreign policy is often in danger of tolerating two critical disjunctions, two failures to connect. First, and most familiar, is that between morality and practicality, ethics and implementation. The second is between the behavior of individuals on the one hand and of governments and states on the other. Once these intricate grids are disconnected, we are groping in moral limbo or simply making angry gestures in the dark. Instead of asking the all-important questions "what is the case?" and "what is to be done?" we are casting about blindly to find out "who is to blame?"

So it is that the new philosophy of ethics could itself be in danger of becoming moralistic rather than truly ethical in its focus, more concerned with politics narrowly defined, more a species of intellectual propaganda than a disinterested study on the basis of everyday precept and conduct of the "right" and the "good." Kant was not alone in his convictions about the practical utility of philosophy or the function of philosophers as guides to action. But his belief was based on the assumption that "the class of philosophers is by nature incapable of plotting and lobbying; it is above suspicion of being made up of propagandists" *(Perpetual Peace,* p. 34).

Inevitably, perhaps, the very rubric "the ethics of public affairs" has an accusatory edge; equally inevitably, most of the time it is governments and statesmen or some anonymous agency who stand accused. "Governments are there to be shot at" is an easily understandable adage at one level; at another it is fundamentally misleading since, morally speaking, in a Western democracy it is the people who put them there who ought to be shot, if the need for shooting arises. At any event, taking shots at governments is essentially the function of journalism. And sure enough, some of the products of the new moral philosophy read as though they were written for the newspapers. Consequently, as philosophy they can lose in ephemerality what they gain in freshness and "relevance."

Calls for a more ethical foreign policy by philosophers, by the press, or by anyone else are fine and good, but only when they are firmly based on the realization that international affairs are not an autonomous activity, largely unrelated to individual states of mind or personal responsibility, the plaything of politicians and interest groups. On the simplest possible level, every practitioner of foreign policy is only too acutely aware that next to the unavoidable uncertainties of international life the greatest constraints or pressures on his actions spring from the ebb and flow in the urges and instincts of domestic opinion. Such constraints can be benign; they can also be disastrous. But for good or ill, that is where a fair proportion of the power and hence the moral responsibility lies. In the nineteenth century, Charles Baudelaire, acutely foreshadowing the changed relationships between governments and individuals in a democratic age, said that government ministers were born for "domestic service to the public" *(Intimate Journals,* p. 74). And if something gets broken, the servants are usually the first to be blamed.

If in appealing for more ethical foreign policies the new philosophers of public affairs are in effect merely calling for a more ethical United States, fine and good too—provided that they indicate the ultimate source of the malady and how the body politic of the country as a whole is to regain its health.

As a non-philosopher, and a non-American, I am unable to pose—let alone answer—any of these questions with the rigor that they deserve and that I admire in the discipline's best representatives—often now in the United States. All I can do is seek to highlight some of the most burning contradictions, coax out some of the central problems, and show why, it seems to me, they have so far been inadequately resolved. It may seem rash to intrude into the territory of jealous professionals, especially when part of their expertise is to pick or talk the other fellow's arguments to pieces. But I am emboldened by the intrepidity with which philosophers intrude into diplomacy.

2

THE
SHOEBLACK
AND THE
SOVEREIGN*

*Surely we must admit that the
same elements and characteristics
that appear in the state must exist
in every one of us. Where else
could they have come from?*
—*PLATO*, **The Republic**

▼

Most people know little or nothing about international affairs, caring more for their own daily lives or domestic circle. The same is true in art, where only small
coteries of aesthetes combine passion with expertise. Yet a

---

*In his *History of the French Revolution* Thomas Carlyle suggested that
it was impossible to place responsibility for the condition of the country
on the eve of the Revolution on single individuals. "Friends, it was every
scoundrel that had lived, and quack-like pretended to be doing, and been
only eating and misdoing, in all provinces of life, as Shoeblack or as Sovereign Lord, each in his degree, from the time of Charlemagne and earlier" (p. 51).

great many people have strong views on both, and the average Philistine is as confident on foreign policy as he is on painting. He knows exactly whom and what he dislikes and can be surprisingly attached to his preferences, given his basic indifference to either genre. He tells you what he thinks about abstract expressionism or East-West relations, Kline or communism, with the peculiar emphasis that springs from strength of moral conviction. He would be deeply offended to be told that, in doing so, he is acting on the basis of the "principle of antipathy," invented by the British utilitarian philosopher, Jeremy Bentham: If you don't like it, it's wrong *(The Principles of Morals and Legislations, Ethical Theories,* p. 375).

Bentham was of course putting a probing finger on a basic human instinct, and his sardonic "principle" operates most unashamedly in areas remote from individual experience, like modern art or foreign affairs, or wherever there is an absence of any clear ethic or aesthetic. In equally uncertain areas of morality or aesthetic value where he has greater personal knowledge, our sturdy Philistine displays a greater reserve, a certain reticence, even some slight nervousness, and more prudently shaded judgments. If he is a man, he has less self-assurance, for example, about what constitutes beauty in a woman: He settles instead for ambiguous adjectives such as "attractive" or, more evasively still, "cute." In sexual morality he is actively or obscurely aware of the pitfalls of dogmatism, instinctively sensing the absence of rigid guidelines in a field where moral confusion is now the rule and laissez-faire—sometimes even anarchy —increasingly the practice. Here too he has his individual prejudices and earthy opinions, but they are tempered by the modulating effects of first-hand experience—experience that teaches him a lot about his own fallibility and that other views are possible besides his own, which he must tolerate if he wishes to remain a social animal.

Yet when it comes to the ethics of foreign policy, much

of this healthy uncertainty evaporates. Whether for the man on the subway or the intellectual in the faculty club more clear-cut notions are deemed to apply. Mists lift, moral perspectives are suddenly sharpened—as though by the very remoteness of the subject—and firm stances are irremovably adopted as instinct is transmuted into principle. In the faculty club and to an extent on the subway too these principles are likely to crystallize into two broad patterns of conviction: "liberal" and "conservative." But almost immediately, definitions begin to blur.

The liberal, although a professional at compassionate understanding, shows little charity towards the very mortal men and women who decide and execute foreign policy in uncharted and unregulated waters beyond their shores and often in situations beyond their power to control. Nor does he have much sympathy for the very real moral dilemmas they face. On the contrary, he is likely to judge practitioners of foreign policy against far more rigorous standards and expect them to exercise greater altruism and self-control than is normal in personal or domestic political life. Nor will the "liberal" be easily persuaded to test the coherence of his convictions on international behavior by placing them in parallel to his views on personal morality. Different categories, he might object. Certainly, one might respond, but not entirely unrelated. Thomas Hobbes was surely right to see humanity in the round as well as in the state of nature, with no water-tight divisions between men's passions and beliefs. And according to Hobbes, "as long as every man holdeth his right of doing anything he liketh, so long are all men in the condition of war" *(Leviathan,* p. 90). The war can be between the sexes, the classes, or whole countries.

Today, in our view of foreign affairs, we seem to have wandered a long way from such central truths and into a maze of contradiction. In the area of sexuality, for example, we are told that the libido is a major determinant of human behavior, with repercussions far beyond the sexual sphere, but also that it is mistaken to expect or to impose any clear moral philosophy—still less rigorous standards—in this crucial domain. At the same time we are frequently reminded—often by the same sources—that among states and the men and women who compose them, sterner ethics apply. Restraint is *de rigueur* in Vietnam but not in San Francisco.

Similarly disconcerting ethical discontinuities are echoed in a different form by conservatively inclined critics of foreign policy at the other end of the faculty club. In contrast to the burning concern of their liberal colleagues, they affect a knowing skepticism, asserting more or less explicitly that in the superior sphere of international relations, all is self-interest, and that familiar notions of decency—misplaced in politics in general—are especially incongruous in dealings among states. At the same time, in a discussion on sexual mores the conservative is more censorious: He is at once the most reluctant to license the libido at home and the most ready to countenance immoral behavior abroad.

While the analogy between sexual and political attitudes is simply the starkest way of highlighting our ingrained and often misleading distinctions between private and public behavior, the conclusion seems inescapable: The liberal asks more of nations than of individuals; the conservative expects more from individuals than nations. But the point is less that "liberals" and "conservatives" both suffer from internal inconsistencies than that these inconsistencies are similar in nature and origin.

The dynamics between these broadly defined cultures are the stuff of everyday controversy in international affairs as elsewhere. It is a debate that engenders much heat and from which many of the participants—journalists, academics, diplomats, politicians, and even occasionally the public—derive much refractive warmth and comfort. But it sheds precious little light on the real ethical problems involved.

A single grand illusion conditions much of what—for the sake of convenience—though admittedly at the risk of some caricature—we might call the Pietist ("liberal") and Brutalist ("conservative") approaches to the morality of foreign policy: Both parties largely deny the existence of a moral continuum between the life of the individual and that of the state, between personal and public behavior—the Brutalists explicitly and the Pietists implicitly. As an unavoidable corollary, both share the equally dubious assumption that international relations are a gigantic swamp of immorality in an otherwise better behaved world.

What this means in practical political terms is that those of either the Pietist or Brutalist persuasion will easily lose touch with human reality because they think of foreign policy as something larger than life, where "outsize" attitudes seem appropriate. In this way, they lose contact with what is practicable and sensible in everyday terms, and adopt moralistic standpoints.

Each group would be dismayed to learn, and unwilling to admit, how much it has in common with the other. But in fact the antithesis between them can be as noisy as it is false, both in regard to the premises from which they begin and in the results that they achieve. A moment's reflection on the superpower relationship makes the point. The Carter administration began with an insufficiently realistic view of the Soviet Union and ended by being more shocked than it should have been by the invasion of Afghanistan, because it had persuaded itself that such actions were no longer in the Russians' nature. The Reagan Presidency began with an equally unrealistic view of the relationship with the Russians—in this case, unrealistically tough. There was never any serious prospect of the administration sustaining the high pitch of ideological hostility of its early years; for one thing the strains on the Atlantic Alliance would have become intolerable. For this and other reasons that hostility began to diminish well before Mikhail Gorbachev arrived on the scene.

Thus, starting from different directions, different administrations edge or stumble towards the same complex reality: The Russians are there and have to be dealt with as they are—not as we would wish them to be—through means that in the end achieve a remarkable similarity: Talk, trade, and the recognition of a shared interest in the avoidance of mutual annihilation.

In foreign as in domestic affairs the "liberal" Pietists have a passion for distributive justice—for cake-sharing rather than cake-baking. This understandable preference for the product of the kitchen rather than its heat involves them in many contradictions. One is that, while insisting on the urgent need to spread the benefits of civil society abroad, they are apt to insist with equal fervor that this benign condition is far from securely established at home. It is hard to see how true brotherhood between nations could precede harmony within each brotherly country. Virtue, one might think, like any other export, will flourish best when the domestic market prospers.

At first sight the Brutalist's vision seems sharper, more cogent, and certainly more convenient. He is apt to see states and statesmen as entirely autonomous phenomena, bound not by ethical rules but by nature itself to obey a single inscrutable and inexorable dynamic: The pursuit of unalloyed self-interest, pure power. Such a stance gives rise to ethical, historical, and practical problems, which can be subsumed in a single objection: It is by no means certain that most countries have always conducted or do in fact today conduct their foreign policies in a moral vacuum. And insofar as they may have done so in the past, it is not clear how far the evidence of history is relevant to our own times.

Whatever the case in former centuries, in a nuclear age, amoral "realism" is no longer realistic.

There are of course degrees of "realism" as of "liberalism"; fortunately, there are liberal realists just as there are realistic libertarians. But in his purer aspect the ideological Brutalist sees foreign policy as ascending above the sordid compromises of everyday life to the plane of higher national interest. Yet whether he knows it or not, he remains as earthbound as his Pietistic liberal partner. Relations among states have no superhuman or mystical dimension: Their dynamics are those that their leaders and population together choose to give them within a given historical inheritance and circumstantial context. Frequently, states behave towards each other neither as badly as the Brutalist seems to wish nor as well as the Pietist seems to hope. On the whole, they conduct themselves little better, or not much worse, than the societies in which their foreign policies take root and evolve. States, in fact, behave rather like individuals or social communities, only rather more so.

This is not to say that there are no differences. In the case of whole nations the implications of an action or of passivity are clearly greater: If things go wrong in the wrong circumstances, war could result. The effects of a mistaken move will be seen more quickly, more visibly, and more dramatically than, for example, the devastating consequences over time of misconceived legislation—or failure to legislate—on road traffic policy, on abortion or divorce, or on alcohol or drug abuse.

There are other dissimilarities. The statesman who steers his country's foreign policy is driving a cumbersome vehicle with defective steering and unreliable brakes. By definition, he is even less in control of events abroad than he is at home. Nor is he ever likely to be short of back-seat drivers: He has a whole truckload, from Philistines to philosophers, each determined to get in his word and to propound enticingly simple or intellectually ingenious solutions. Meanwhile, the vehicle lumbers on along inadequately policed roads, mined at regular intervals.

To impress foreigners, his electorate, and himself, the statesman will try to camouflage any feelings of uncertainty by displaying greater confidence than he feels or than the situation warrants. He knows that any mistakes and their moral implications will be magnified and silhouetted by the media to make the perpetrator—or victim of circumstance—appear in a grotesque light. At times, there may be compensations too: The chance to cast a fine and noble shadow when the back-drop happens to come right. But in normal periods the odds against lasting foreign policy "successes," as distinct from the occasional conference or summit meeting, are even heavier than in the domestic sphere.

In a democracy the pursuit of international relations is particularly hazardous. In a Western country foreign affairs involve on the one side decisions made on the basis of incomplete, inaccurate, outdated, or willfully distorted information by preoccupied men or women under pressure from allies and adversaries, political opponents and cabinet colleagues, generals, finance ministers, pressure groups, intellectuals, public opinion, and the media; on the other side, more or less competent diplomats, operating in different time zones, cultures, and tongues and against a background of historically accumulated fears and suspicions, must execute these decisions. With the best will in the world—also sometimes wanting—there is scope for miscalculation. But whatever the combination of circumstances, there is likely to be precious little practical room for moral absolutism. Each element in every decision is likely to be impure and the sum total contaminated by every sort of self-interest, enlightened or otherwise, and ethical *a priori*.

But is this so surprising? Here we come back to more familiar ground and more common experience: These complexities and ethical hazards are merely a magnification of dilemmas faced by individuals or societies at a much humbler level. The "solutions" or evasions to which governments resort are a manifestation of everyday moral compromises at the level of state. In no sense are they beyond the understanding or the field of ethical responsibility of the simple citizen.

There is abundant evidence for this moral continuum at every level, from theoretical discussion to daily observation. But perhaps the best example is a negative one, drawn from history. Philosophers of ethics, from Aristotle in Greece in the fourth-century B.C. to G. E. Moore in early twentieth-century England have all lamented the difficulty of defining notions of good and evil, and some more modern thinkers have suggested that it is time to give up the struggle. But this difficulty is part of the whole human condition. It is not confined to relations among states or to those who formulate and execute foreign policy.

The lack of clear definitions of good and evil does not mean that we have been wandering in an ethical desert for centuries with no theoretical stars to guide us; on the contrary, we have had theories without number. But such nostrums as philosophers have evolved were nearly always specifically or inherently universal; whatever their merits, they must be seen as applying quite naturally to nations as much as to those who composed them.*

In a field where guidance offered by the "experts" has been so notoriously imprecise and inconstant, common sense and practical experience of the nature of the relationship between private and public ethics assume even greater importance than usual. Both by intuition and observation,

---

*One exception are the historicists, who began with G. W. F. Hegel and who tie their understanding of ethics to communities, giving a particular nation a "world historical" role, thus leaving aside the international dimension—a handy stance for anyone who aspires to be a Pietist at home and a Brutalist abroad.

we know that there is no essential moral distinction between the behavior of individuals, who may seek domination over each other for its own sake or in defense of their interests, and that of states, where "self-protection" leads so frequently to self-aggrandizement. Industrial disputes, like conflicts between countries, display a naked element of pure power that neither side attempts to disguise. The rhetoric, pressures, and techniques of negotiation used to resolve them are in all essentials similar to those used in international affairs. There is bluff, there are lock-outs ("breaking of relations"), there are deals and reconciliation. Force can count too, and the results of battles on picket lines (even though they may be as symbolic as some of the wars of the eighteenth century) play their roles in the outcomes.

It helps to clarify the links between the behavior of governments abroad and individuals at home if we contrast the greater realism in domestic policies.

In domestic affairs politicians are not seriously expected to keep all their election promises, in letter or even sometimes in spirit: People realize that circumstances change—oil prices are a nice example—and that manifestos are often little more than the expression of an ideal. Yet international statesmen sometimes seem to be expected to abide more rigorously by their agreements, even when they are clearly overtaken by events. There are excellent reasons for greater caution in the field of foreign affairs, where the consequences of cynicism could be more dire. But the difference is quantitative, not qualitative.

Not all parallels among private, public, and international behavior are so negative or dispiriting. In foreign relations, as in civil society, progress is not unknown. Just as there have been some social and political advances in ordering domestic or industrial affairs since, say, the twenties, so there have been signs of parallel improvements in the behavior of the international community. Conciliation among social classes has some counterpart in cooperation within and among regional groups of countries. The incidence of war and its relative destructiveness are studies in themselves. But contrary to conventional wisdom or passing impression, the aggregate of international conflict today is by no means at a historically high level. The same is true, in the West at least, of strikes. Thus to press the parallels between domestic and international behavior is not to resign oneself to a Hobbesian pessimism about human nature or to anarchy.

Some of these truths may seem self-evident. It would be odd indeed if any progress in social ethics at home were to go hand in hand with a decline in comparative areas of international behavior or vice versa. Yet, obvious though they may seem, time and again one encounters an implicit reluctance to recognize these organic relationships.

In discussing events at home and abroad, people by and large adopt a despairing tone in the case of international relations, a certain doom-laden resignation, as if it were in this field that man is ever to be seen at his worst. In a century that has seen in its first half two devastating world wars and is overshadowed in its second by nuclear tensions —not to speak of the sharp divisions between hunger and plenty—there is no difficulty in finding grounds for despondency. But these conditions alone are not sufficient to explain the almost willful pessimism that is commonly assumed in international affairs and for which there is no ready analogue in our domestic lives. Again, there is a gloomy identity of view between our Pietist and Brutalist: Both tend to assume the worst, sometimes despite the evidence. The same Stygian mood pervades the work of many political scholars and philosophers and other experts in the field, whatever their political convictions. Like the media, whose superficialities it is their business to transcend, moral philosophers in particular have a pronounced tendency to concentrate on the abnormal, the egregious and the infamous in international affairs (wars, genocide, massacres, or espionage) to an even greater degree than at home.

To some extent this is a *déformation professionelle,* resulting partly perhaps from an aspiration to scientific status through the decisive clash of example and counter-example. Maybe the explanation is more simple: Possibly our experts are just looking for stimulating ingredients to spice a theory or distract a reader. In any event, the result can be the impression that, while moral philosophers prosper and grow plump on grand or exquisite ethical dilemmas, the plainer fare—the routine management of foreign policy—is left fastidiously to one side. Partly as a result, foreign affairs have more than their quota of Krafft Ebings and not enough general practitioners who deal with the common cold. Nations, like people, do indeed behave perversely, and the results of collective perversity are more visible. But it is questionable whether the incidence of morbidity in states is higher than elsewhere. Despite what the newspapers and learned articles sometimes appear to suggest, war is not the norm; diplomacy to prevent it is.

Whence, then, diplomacy's reputation for amorality, not to say unique wickedness? Is it a legacy of the wars and nationalisms of the past, when cynicism was deemed essential for the maintenance of security (though in fact things were never so simple)? Is it a folk-memory of the legendary ruthlessness of Charles-Maurice de Talleyrand, Klemens Metternich, Otto von Bismarck? Is it the result of something deeper—a form of collective guilt, fear, or assertiveness, assuaged by rounding on the diplomats or practitioners of foreign affairs, who are alternately accused of unprincipled compromise, bungling ineptitude, or dangerous risk-taking?

The language in which the debate on foreign policy is conducted is in itself revealing. The whole subject suffers from linguistic and therefore moral inflation well beyond what might be reasonably expected. The most mundane problems become "issues" smothered in overtones of high principle even more quickly than in domestic affairs. The vocabulary of foreign policy discussion or even presidential or prime-ministerial speeches sets the tone.

Straightforward, more or less enlightened pursuit of self-interest tends to become a matter of destiny, "national" in France, for example, or "manifest" in the United States. Similarly, empirical groping in the dark, which is how most statesmen spend much of their time, is invariably interpreted as tactical maneuvering. Anything remotely consistent—such as two consecutive steps in the same direction, however faltering—becomes a "strategy" (often "brilliant"), elaborated after deep reflection by far-seeing statesmen. A more sophisticated public-relations policy by the new Soviet leader, Mikhail Gorbachev, following a long period of indifference to or even contempt for international opinion, is instantly construed as a master plan to seduce the West.

Much of this is mere media hyperbole. But it carries more interesting implications. The major attraction of the moral inflation of foreign policy is that it facilitates moral evasion and the flight from the grinding and thankless task of seeking realistic solutions. The language of "issues," on which virtuous people "feel strongly" or to which they are "totally committed," is often no more than a heavy smoke-screen for fugitives from moral responsibility. "Confronting an issue" is a far more attractive proposition than seeking the resolution of a problem. The same holds good in domestic policy; but "issues" seem to increase in size and number with distance and intractability—the "Third World" being the most obvious example. To cite one instance, for many years Rhodesia was the major "issue" in British foreign policy, and people of all persuasions found it an extremely attractive stick with which to beat each other. When a solution was found, there was a discernible note of regret amongst the applause. For many, the Rhodesian problem had been a welcome distraction from challenges posed by the economic and social decline of Britain during the same period.

The whole image of diplomacy is one of swollen contrasts: Between pomp and mendacity, suaveness and cynicism, social elegance and moral turpitude. All this ties in neatly with the assumption that international affairs are a scene of debased values; and when events fail to live up to the inflated rhetoric, as they almost invariably do, it is a matter of profound satisfaction to critics of all persuasions and descriptions.

And so we come to the central problem: If indeed it is true that the ethical inferiority of international affairs is largely a convenient fiction, *cui bono?* Obviously, the critics have an interest. The statesman himself, however, is among the first to benefit from sustaining the illusion: In a field of highly restrictive constraints, what he needs above all is greater freedom of action, a longer ethical leash. He can hardly say as much and instead will collude with one strain of public opinion in the pretense that in international relations a higher morality operates. The words of course mean exactly the opposite of what they seem to say, and everyone knows it: They mean, in effect, the suspension of familiar norms of conduct in the supreme interests of the state. A "higher morality," in other words, is a pretext for lower morals.

The media, with their perennial interest in heightening the chiaroscuro of the news bulletin, benefit too from playing their part in the pretense. The closer the story is to the moral equivalent of a Caravaggio painting, all fierce contrasts and spotlit drama, the happier they will be. There are clear attractions to everyone in presenting international affairs in terms of Punch and Judy morality, concentrating on the sheer outlandishness of abroad and suggesting implicitly that "normal" ethics cannot and do not hold sway there.

As for the elector, he will respond predictably as the

balloon of moral inflation is alternately launched and punctured; it all underlines his fundamental assumption, nourished by spy movies and bad novels, that foreign policy is and always will be an exception to normal standards of behavior, a field dominated by smooth villains and the necessity of violence. Occasionally, in the face of what is presented to him as a particularly striking piece of infamy that goes against his nation's interest or damages its reputation, he will protest his shock and dismay—and then will proclaim equally loudly his powerlessness as an individual to affect the course of events.

Students of foreign policy profit from the fiction too: Whatever their politics, they share the interest of the statesman in adding a high moral tone to what can easily become a humdrum, journalistic subject.

Yet whatever the voter or media-man might affect to believe, to enter the foreign ministry of an average democracy is not to set foot in a zone of ethical extra-territoriality. Like other humans, diplomats—and even sometimes statesmen—may retain what that great skeptic, the eighteenth-century British philosopher David Hume, called "some particle of the lamb, kneaded into their frame alongside the elements of the wolf and the serpent" *(An Enquiry Concerning The Principles of Morals, Ethical Theories,* p. 303.) Many diplomats lead tediously blameless lives. If some affect a glossy cynicism, it is less because cynicism is inherent in their function than because it seems to be expected of them.

One of the reasons diplomats sometimes enjoy playing up to their image of miniature, modern Machiavellis is their very impatience at pressure to develop a more "moral" foreign policy. But the best diplomat is a realist in the best sense: He knows that his is the unenviable task of integrating ethics with practice and that no one at home or abroad will allow him to forget the limits of the possible. Like the statesman, he may well yearn for greater freedom of action,

but also for a public that is more informed about the complex realities of foreign policy—though not perhaps to the
point of wanting the public to become too directly associated
with its elaboration or execution. He will certainly be uncomfortably aware that, as things stand today, public "concern" is liable to be expressed most frequently in bouts of
unhealthy moralism, flaring up sporadically in times of
stress or crisis, and that emotional conflagrations are especially likely to occur during national inquests on what are
seen as foreign policy failures: Suez in the United Kingdom,
Vietnam in the United States.

It is at such times that the electorate is suddenly
brought face to face with its own responsibilities; not unnat-
urally, it finds the experience disagreeable. Having elected,
or allowed to be elected, the succession of presidents who
pursued American involvement in Southeast Asia to its bitter end, the public was in a spot. Insofar as it feels collective
remorse, or moral confusion, it will seek to work it off in
predictable ways. Spokesmen will be found, in politics or
the press, to pursue this self-chastisement and to exorcise
the national guilt. Predictably too, those of the "Pietist"
persuasion will be in the fore in this exercise. Things will
probably go too far, either out of simple excess or political
ambition, quickly reaching the point where, in Karl Jaspers's phrase, "morality becomes suspect for purely moral
reasons" *(Nietzsche,* p. 147).

Such spasms of moral despair do little to promote ethics
in public life and have an unpleasant habit of provoking
counter-reactions. In the case of Vietnam, patriotism—with
its inevitable admixture of chauvinism—soon reasserted
itself with a vengeance: The history of American foreign
policy in the last fifteen years and some of the avoidable
East-West tensions we have lived through surely demonstrate the point beyond reasonable doubt.

Foreign affairs are prosecuted for and by the man or
woman in the crowd. In practice, of course, the situation is

less simple, and in the average Western democracy the growing importance of the media introduces a new factor, which to some extent exculpates the individual. Both electorate and statesman are swayed by its influence and seek to harness its power. The ethical responsibilities of the media themselves are easily overlooked in the process. They are even less easily definable than the other ingredients in the formulation of foreign policy; but that is no reason for granting press, radio, and television a sort of moral dispensation.

It is equally the case that the power or impotence of an individual in a given situation will be deeply affected by the structures of the institution or agency that employs him. Yet whatever happens on the way, the chain of command and accountability in foreign as in domestic affairs starts and stops with an individual, be he voter, bureaucrat, or cabinet minister; another plain truth perhaps, but one that is too rarely spoken in an age where there is a tendency to take refuge in group dynamics, whether of the constituency, "the community," the cabinet room, or of vaguely defined collective "rights."

What this means in practice can be simple but also very significant. The thirteen million Frenchmen who voted for General Charles de Gaulle in 1965 entitled him to claim, more prosaically than he might have put it at the time, that he *was* the State: *l'état, c'est moi*. With his Brutalist tendencies, de Gaulle was in the habit of enveloping rather humdrum statements of fact in dramatic Gallic hyperbole. It is of little consequence whether one applauds or deplores his policies; his subsequent successes and failures were those of a majority of Frenchmen.

For exactly equivalent reasons the stance of an American president on nuclear matters or military spending, with all their domestic and international repercussions, is the responsibility of the populace who put him there—even more, in a sense, than his own. His mistakes, excesses, or sheer unpredictability reflect the will, or indecision, of the electorate. (In modern times, with modern communications, the point could even be stretched to include non-democracies that can now be reached by foreign broadcasts: After the U.S. air raid on Libya in April, 1986, a Voice of America broadcast to the Libyans stated, not unpersuasively: "Colonel Qadaffi is your head of state. So long as you obey his orders, you must bear the consequences.")

The problem of the ethical accountability of groups of individuals is clearly more serpentine than these few lines suggest. It is easy to sympathize with the difficulties of jurists and philosophers in handling the concept of the responsibilities of whole societies. But it is a debate that can become almost willfully abstruse. Sometimes one is tempted to respond as Samuel Johnson did to the insistence of Bishop Joseph Berkeley, the eighteenth-century thinker, on the insubstantiality of matter: Johnson simply kicked his foot against a stone. By ignoring the simple reality of the link between governors and the governed in a twentieth-century democracy, some theorists are ignoring primary political matter: Try kicking, instead of Dr. Johnson's stone, a cabinet minister or, still better, an elector . . .

Our unhealthy reluctance to bring the individual face to face with his or her own moral duties in a democratic society reflects the lingering primitive need of communities for more visible and easily accessible moral scapegoats. However frustrating it may be for us, the fact is that in our late twentieth-century democracies, we are no longer able to grumble at princes; we have only ourselves to blame.

One of the characteristic illusions of the twentieth century is that all problems are supposed to be capable of solution once they are broken down into their component parts and handed over to the appropriate specialists. The morality of international affairs is no exception. Yet it would be wrong to expect too much from specialist studies in the field, remarkable as some of these have been. The innate tendency already noted to isolate the behavior of individuals from that of states is an example of such compartmentalization at work. If morality is both indivisible and peculiarly hard to define in meaningful, commonly accepted terms at all, to write convincingly on international ethics becomes even more problematical than to write on ethics *tout court*. Isolating the ethical atom in our decisions is hard enough; splitting it neatly between public and private elements is virtually impossible for the excellent reason that Plato gives: The same elements and characteristics that appear in the state appear in every one of us.

None of this is an argument for abandoning the attempt to improve our understanding of the ethics of foreign policy. A glance at the international stage is enough to remind us of the perennial need for such understanding. But it is a good reason for looking back for a moment beyond the increasingly over-refined studies on the subject and to reconsider the problems in the light of earlier ages' conclusions about man's moral nature.

Our nuclear predicament may be unprecedented, but our search for workable moral precepts is not. Yet when we look back, the most striking aspect of moral philosophy as a whole is its failure to provide coherent, practical, or lasting ethical systems for public or private behavior. Given that fact and our insistence that the conduct of states cannot be divorced from that of individuals, it would be wrong to expect too much guidance from the past in the field of international relations. Unlike the position in the natural sciences, in foreign affairs there is no steady accumulation of wisdom and certainly no ready-made blueprints to resolve today's dilemmas.

But for a generation as historically introverted as our own, the very contemplation of the intellectual struggles of moral philosophers in previous centuries induces a healthy prudence and humility about our own contemporary judgments, especially since their failures were by no means total. By adopting an unashamedly eclectic approach, it is even possible to piece together a serviceable craft from the hulks of classical ethical theory and other areas of philosophy, reinforcing it with our own knowledge of current practice. The planks will not always fit together well, and the boat will never be completely watertight. But in a field where coherence seems unobtainable and perhaps even undesirable, this should not worry us unduly. We must salvage wisdom where we can.

Some figures—such as Immanuel Kant—command immediate attention. Kant's main works do not encourage us to think of him as a pragmatic guide to foreign policy (*The Critique of Pure Reason* seemed so obscure that he had to reformulate the argument to make it more intelligible to scholars). Nor was he notably experienced in the ways of the world: He never left his native town of Königsberg, let alone travelled aboard. Least of all does his system of ethical imperatives sound at first as if it could cast much light on the murky conundrums of foreign affairs.

Yet, in fact, Kant was a highly practical thinker and in the soundest meaning of the term, a realist. Although untravelled, as a democrat he understood the aims of the French Revolution, though he was appalled by the Terror. Unlike many other moral philosophers, he wrote specifically on foreign affairs, where he combined good judgment with far-sighted vision. He advocated a federation of free states and was a supporter of the United States, as he would have been of the European Economic Community.

This unusual pragmatism went along with a system of ethical absolutes that set a barrier against the archenemy of all morality—naked expediency. His "categorical imperative" insists that all our actions should be based on respect for human beings as ends in themselves. This notion is especially relevant to the conduct of nations in the nuclear age where the first priority is the self-preservation of the species, and to the modern emphasis on the rights of the individual.

Today, one of the leading American philosophers, Willard Van Orman Quine, has an obvious claim to our attention. It is not immediately evident how the work of a twentieth-century mathematical logician can be yoked together with that of an eighteenth-century German idealist, especially since Quine has written little about ethics and less about international affairs. But one of the main contentions in his work—that meaning can only be deduced from a given context—can be seen as complementary to Kant, who also made it clear that universal principles need to be interpreted in a particular framework. If one thinks of morality, like meaning, as discernible largely only from a set of circumstances, though also underpinned by indestructible principles, Kantian absolutes begin to illuminate the Quinean context, like theater lights on a stage. Obvious examples today would be the overriding duty of statesmen to avoid the risk of edging inadvertently closer to nuclear conflict in the routine management of a troublesome aspect of East-West relations, or to work for the elimination of institutional racism within confines that will not provoke wider conflicts.

Many practitioners of foreign policy would instinctively shy away from philosophic abstractions, partly through a bluff resistance to intellectualism, partly through overwhelming preoccupation with the routine pressures of the moment. Yet in a rational world there is no conceivable conflict between the abstract and the concrete—that is what the "contextual" view is about. In the last analysis, the two are inseparable. "The pressure of business," which helps us to shun abstraction, is, as in our daily lives, also a form of escape.

It would be equally wrong to escape the humbler context—the ethics of the everyday, the morality of the mo-

ment. It is this that is most revealing and ultimately determinant. It is in the filigree of habit, of daily decisions on
minor matters, of the practice of democracy itself that underlying principles—or absence of principle—can emerge
most clearly. It is often in routine affairs too that the potential for conflict or conciliation lies, rather than in some permanent dialogue where fundamental tenets are sharply
defined and eloquently disputed.

This is where the current emphasis on practical ethics
can produce a healthy corrective—providing it avoids over-
balancing in another direction and becoming a mere vehicle
for political engagement. The ideal—to infuse discussion of
contemporary foreign policy problems with a morally
harder and historically deeper spirit—is easy to state but
demanding to achieve.

Viewed in this light and against this fuller background,
morality becomes less a matter of rigid tenets and more a
patchwork of actions woven on a loom of principle in which
we hope that an agreeable pattern will emerge over time.
However often we step back to review progress, it would be
naive to think that a particular moral task will ever be done
or the pattern completed. Sisyphus' fate of endlessly rolling
a stone up a hill symbolizes the problem: We should think
in terms of what he might have produced over an age or two
if he were to take a rest from his rock and take up spinning
instead.

The very incompleteness of our moral lives gives scope
for cautious optimism. Seen in this light, much modern diplomacy begins to seem less negative and disreputable than
is sometimes imagined. Its efforts are mainly devoted to the
avoidance rather than the pursuit of conflict. Inevitably, its
small triumphs are as newsworthy as crime prevention, and
the containment of conflict inevitably involves compromise—which runs the risk of seeming unethical to the
Pietist or Brutalist.

But it is difficult to deny that some statesmen pursue

constructive and worthy goals by perfectly respectable—if rarely wholly selfless—means. Even where economic motives are paramount, this can further the general welfare by its stimulus to world trade. Samuel Johnson's view that a man is rarely so harmlessly employed as in making money can be applied more persuasively to the activities of modern Western states than Lenin's dictum that the capitalist struggle for markets inevitably brings war.

In the construction of Europe, with its gradual accumulation of common legislation, cultural identity, and political purpose, the advantages of a piecemeal over a prescriptive international "morality" can be seen to its best advantage. In terms of the avoidance of conflict there can be few more persuasive examples. Gradualist patterns of cooperation have the virtue of attainability. A concrete "regional morality" does not preclude wider principles or goals. It is not divorced from universalism, but represents progress towards it. This is surely preferable to a high-minded but abstract "global ethic," especially where it replaces a local tradition of rivalry and warfare. Ethics means custom, and custom, in the words of the poet W. B. Yeats is "the spreading laurel tree" ("A Prayer for my Daughter," p. 211).

Progress has not been dizzy, and such positive developments as have taken place—especially in Europe—have sometimes been obtained under the umbrella of a broader security system, depending heavily on the United States. But this more earth-creeping approach to the building of international relationships has already enjoyed a better future than the "total solutions" of global cooperation—the "outlawing" of war by the Kellog-Briand Pact in 1925 or the grand but still hollow edifice of the United Nations itself. There is little early likelihood of the nation-state dissolving its personality in this amorphous entity, which includes one country of one billion and another of less than one hundred inhabitants. It is no source of satisfaction that there are far more dead letters in the documents signed in San Francisco in 1945 than in the Treaty of Rome, which established the Common Market twelve years later; but it is a fact.

Clearly, regionalism too has its moral pitfalls. It would be wrong and ill-advised for Europe to cultivate her own garden to the exclusion of wider considerations—by artificially inflating agricultural production on the assumption that Africa must remain doomed to perpetual hunger, for example. Regionalism cannot be exclusive, any more than ethics: It must remain part of a wider pattern of security and prosperity. Nor can it exclude aspirations toward higher or broader forms of international association. The United Nations must remain a goal, even if it is not yet a fully functioning institution.

There is a good deal of complementarity in the universalist and regional ethics: The principles regulating relations between states enunciated in the United Nations' Charter are nowhere better applied than in the member countries in the European Economic Community. This is because they are applied among like-minded nations, for the best—that is the most rational—motives: An immediate, intelligently perceived self-interest, merging inextricably into the collective long-term interest of the region as a whole. It is difficult to bind nations, or individuals, by the iron bands of absolutist ethics; but they can be restrained by the silken thread of cooperation in self-interest.

For reasons too diverting to explore, the expression "moral character" has become outmoded. Yet it is immediately clear to us what the phrase means, and it still has a positive ring about it. In particular it suggests an energetic, outward-looking disposition, displayed not in hyperactivity but in hard work and contact with harsh external realities. By definition, states have moral characteristics too, and it is a handy rule of thumb that the countries that are least "moral" in their international behavior are those with completely closed societies, or those tempted by introversion.

One of the most troubling developments in Western

countries in recent years has been the growth of isolationist pressures on both sides of the Atlantic, notably in the United Kingdom and the United States. In Britain these temptations have tended to stem in part from a cultural and economic world-weariness, a condition that may be in the process of being reversed. In the United States, they have their source in domestic self-doubt, in foreign policy frustrations, and in the apparent incomprehension of American policy by her Allies. The symptoms can differ widely, but defense is a good touchstone. In Britain the Labour Party's decision to dispense with nuclear weapons and American nuclear protection reflects not just naive idealism but the moral fatigue of one section of British opinion with the whole costly, complex question of defense: A shrinking away from the stern imperatives of deterrence and shared responsibilities for maintaining a balance. It is a decision that reflects a yearning—fortunately not yet widespread—that international realities might somehow go away and leave Britain in peace. In the United States the parallel illusion of autarchy has recently taken the form of a vision of invincibility based on a combination of massive offensive and defensive potential.

In countries, as with individuals, we do not associate "moral character," however defined, with moral introversion, however displayed. Each country's diplomacy, like each personality, has a certain "moral tone"—not in a priggish but in a tough practical sense, since real morality is a harshly functional business. There is nothing either practical or ethical about the star-gazing of the Pietist or the Brutalist's heroic despair.

PRINCIPLED PRACTICE

3

> *In a democracy which does not respect the intellectual life, and is not guided by it, demagogy has full play and the level of national life is depressed to that of the ignorant and uncultivated.*
> —*THOMAS MANN,* The Coming Victory of Democracy

▼

Modern statesmen rarely seek to justify their actions in terms of classical moral theory or to reflect, in public at least, on its lessons. Given the ease with which our modern leaders would find in underpinning their actions by the selective quotation of some great name or theory, the omission is not wholly to be regretted. As distinct from statesmen of previous centuries, ours are likely both to be less inclined and to have less time to read much at all—let alone write. Despite his dislike of "morbid" debate, Thomas Jefferson combined an active political life with the pursuit of philosophy; few statesmen today could do the same. Still fewer would be capable of producing a one-hundred page pamphlet as William Gladstone did in 1876 on *The Bulgarian Horrors and the Question of the East*—the burning moral question of the day. Even if they did, the response from the public might be quizzical. Their works would be unlikely to become best-sellers, as Gladstone's did, or to bring down a government on a moral issue.

An even more fundamental question than whether statesmen should speculate on the ethics of foreign policy is whether closer acquaintance with ethical theories would breed more ethical politicians. There are different views on how much is to be gained by the abstract knowledge of moral precepts. Plato thought that it would be helpful for the rulers of men to be acquainted with the idea of the "good" simply to help them decide between right and wrong. Likewise, Kant (who once accused politicians of understanding *men* but not *man)* lamented the failure of those in government to heed the advice of professional thinkers. On the other hand, some would argue that men of action would do well to resist any temptations to seek wisdom or guidance in the writings of moral philosophers. Aristotle warned against expecting too much enlightenment from outside "experts" of any sort. He put the issue another way: Good judgment in ethics can only be made by people whose moral habits are already excellent. This is less shallow and circular than it sounds, as the philosopher's astute remark that "even medical men do not seem to be made by the study of a text book" shows. (Since Aristotle himself was a court physician, the comment is more than a mere analogy.) But modern politicians might conclude that it is less than wholly satisfying to be told that statesmen who do a good job are moral statesmen.

David Hume, the eighteenth-century English skeptic, added a further disincentive to the man of action in search of moral enlightenment when he remarked that "the more we habituate ourselves to an accurate scrutiny of morals, the more delicate feeling do we acquire of the most minute distinctions between vice and virtue" *(An Enquiry Concerning the Principles of Morals, p. 294)*. The average politician might understandably consider poring over moral minutiae to be hardly conducive to his main task—to make decisions—and prefer to rely instead on the more congenial advice of the instant political moralizers in his entourage.

Furthermore, philosophers themselves have often recognized that the study of ethics is particularly elusive and have frankly admitted the difficulty of evolving clear and coherent systems. Aristotle warned that "we must be satisfied with a broad outline of the truth" *(The Nicomachean Ethics, p. 65)*. Hume made a positive start but fell back into his familiar "diffidence and skepticism" *(An Enquiry, p. 307)*. Bentham explained with engaging robustness in his *Principles of Morals and Legislation,* that it was both unnecessary and impossible to prove his own main utilitarian principles of moral behavior. Moore said that you cannot explain what "good" is, any more than what "yellow" is *(Principia Ethica, p. 14)*.

The very elusiveness of the subject can easily lead to misinterpretation. Moore's *Principia Ethica* repudiated definitions and based morality on simple, unanalyzable principles that were supposed to be objects of intuition. Bernard Williams has called this a higher form of silliness. Moore's book certainly had some strange effects: It is thought, for example, to have been widely mistaken by intellectuals of the time—not least by the Bloomsbury set—for an invitation to sexual license. The risks of similar misunderstanding by statesmen are staggering. It is not difficult to imagine them getting it into their heads that Kant's emphasis on the *a priori* is another way of stressing the importance of instincts—a highly gratifying message to politicians who are mostly convinced of the unique efficiency of their own.

Should statesmen still persevere in philosophical inquiry in the face of so much self-doubt by the experts themselves across the years, they would face new frustrations. In the English-speaking world, where utilitarian thinking has invaded so much of the political debate, discussion about ethics can be couched so much in the free, elastic, and inexact idiom of the day that this discussion can lead anywhere and justify almost anything.

On the other hand, there are some modern writers whose works are insulated by hermetic technicalities from common parlance and sometimes common sense. Statesmen would quickly become impatient with the way such writers express themselves and would be slow to see the relevance to their own pressing dilemmas of their frequent resort to paradox and unreal ethical conundrums. They would find themselves obliged to grapple with a new and opaque terminology, far removed from their own stout certainties. But there could be agreeable surprises too. They would be pleased to discover, for example, that they had been practicing "act-deontology"—deciding each moral problem separately instead of applying general rules—when they thought they had simply been making the best of things. "Situation ethics," as such theories are called, would have a guilty appeal for the politician in a hurry for a quick fix.

One consolation would be that the further they went back in time, the more accessible the prose, from David Hume's elegant and persuasive concision to the Socratic dialogues themselves. Another might be the revelation of the extent of the divergences among the experts—always a source of keen satisfaction to politicians, in ethics as in economics.

Despite all the obstacles, the relevance of moral theory to the very real world of politicians should be beyond doubt, though it seems a pious hope indeed that many would tear themselves away from the ticker-tape long enough to rediscover this truism. Were they to do so, they would find in philosophical discussion, even at its most impenetrable, striking reflections of the difficulties they face in decision taking in the hard, contemporary world. Philosophers did not write in an historical void, and their writings influenced, and were influenced by, the events of the time. The informed speculations of gifted men are part of inherited "reality" too. In less utilitarian terms, simply to read such authors is to cultivate not just a salutary humility, but what Marcel Proust called "the good manners of the mind"—a quality that today for some reason is thought incongruous in political leaders.

For makers or simply executors of foreign policy, there are obvious difficulties in developing this quality. One is the sheer volume of what might be read; another the density of the matter; a third the difficulty of untrained minds in penetrating it. Unavoidably, the mere practitioner will discover that his own chance experience, and the conclusions he draws from it, will influence both his selection of reading and his reaction to what he reads. He lives in a different world—the world of action—and probably at a different time from the thinkers whose abstractions he seeks to fathom. The most he can hope for is the occasional spark across the historical or vocational gap: A sudden contact between the small sights he has seen and what large minds have thought, from which some flicker of illumination may flow. For better or for worse, the thinkers whose work has set the spark crackling in my case are Hobbes, Machiavelli, Kant, the utilitarians, Willard Van Orman Quine, and—in a more negative sense—John Rawls.

As author of *The Leviathan,* with its famous description of life as "solitary, poor, nasty, brutish and short," there would seem little doubt about which camp Thomas Hobbes would join in any debate on the morality of international affairs. He had a poor view of the moral proclivities of individuals and thought no better of states. His own life was neither brutish nor short—he lived to eighty-five—though a little solitary. Symbolically enough, it began with an international trial of strength: He was born prematurely when his mother was startled by the report of the approach of the Spanish Armada.

At first sight, Hobbes's whole doctrine seems to come perilously close to the view that "might is right." He does not expect too much from human conduct: Left to himself in the state of nature, every man will be at war against every man. War would be like the weather, and peace merely fine interludes for which we would have to be thankful:

> *For as the nature of foul weather lieth not in a shower or two or rain, but in an inclination thereto of many days together, so the nature of war consists not in actual fighting, but in the known disposition thereto, during all the time there is no assurance to the contrary. All other time is peace.* (Leviathan, *p. 186*)

Hobbes's description of the human predisposition to conflict is distressingly persuasive; today we might call it an uncompromising statement of the realities of the situation. There is little difficulty in accommodating the term "cold war" to his meteorological image. In the light of experience since his time, it seems difficult to dissent from the view that the general inclination of people and states appears to be towards "a perpetual and restless desire for power after power" *(Leviathan,* p. 161); that countries as a matter of course have "their weapons pointing, and their eyes fixed on one another" *(Leviathan,* p. 188); and that, when conflict comes, "force and fraud are, in war, the two cardinal virtues" *(Leviathan,* p. 188).

Hobbes's conclusion is that only the surrender of the individual means of self-preservation to political absolutism, as an act of self-protection against one's fellows and the nation's enemies, will ensure domestic peace. Although he does not say so directly, in international terms this can only be a recipe for spheres of influence controlled by great powers or, alternatively, the surrender of all power to a single Leviathan. There seems a striking coincidence between his belief that individuals should be ready to abandon a portion of their freedom in exchange for protection and Leonid Brehznev's infamous doctrine of the "limited sovereignty" of Communist states under the Soviet aegis. In practice, this means of course that the countries of Eastern Europe are free only to remain indefinitely as members of the Warsaw Pact and protectorates of Moscow. Hobbes would presumbably point out—quite correctly—that in the case of Communist states, these protectorates did not come about voluntarily and that their choice of protectors would not be a rational one since the countries in question, left to themselves, could have evolved alternative security arrangements.

Hobbes's catastrophic view of human nature and his recommendations for centralized coercive power to force man to conform to any "social compact" can hardly recommend him to our democratic sensibilities. Nor is his climatological doctrine on the inevitability of war a very practical message in a nuclear century. It is some time since Communist China abandoned the view that nuclear war is as unavoidable as rain. Now the superpowers are also coming to terms with the fact that the vagaries of the political atmosphere must not be allowed to precipitate a nuclear confrontation.

The main contemporary objection to Hobbes is that his ethical prescriptions are purely rational and prudential and do not spring from any recognition of natural liberty or moral claims. This is one reason they are often said not to cover the contingency of nuclear weapons. Yet Hobbes is not nearly as simplistic a thinker nor as relentless a pessimist as he is sometimes portrayed. In a sense, he is ahead of us, arguing in one of the most perceptive passages of *The Leviathan* that it is ultimately this very "natural liberty," based on the natural equality of man, that is at the root of our problems: "From this equality of ability, ariseth the equality of hope in the attaining of our ends. And therefore if any two men desire the same thing, which nevertheless they cannot both enjoy, they become enemies" *(Leviathan,* p. 186). In other words, we are sufficiently equal to be mutually vulnerable—an aspect of Hobbes's thinking that does begin to cover the nuclear contingency. The idea that much of our troubles stem from this equality, rather than wrongly assumed or imposed inequalities, is unlikely to find much favor today and is clearly less true of states of different sizes than of individuals. But a glance at the performance of the United Nations, where votes in the General Assembly are technically of the same weight (even though membership of the Security Council is loaded to reflect international realities) suggests that, however much we may dislike his conclusions, a good deal of Hobbes's thinking is still pretty close to "the realities of the situation"—certainly closer than the views of some of the ethical idealists of our own time. The problems he poses, especially about the disadvantages of strict equality, have obvious implications for the extension of international law.

Hobbes may have been rather hard on human nature, but we should not be too hard on Hobbes. There is an enlightened side to this hyper-realist. To describe man's predisposition to conflict is not to preach war; in fact, Hobbes's first law of nature is "to seek peace, and follow it" *(Leviathan,* p. 190). It is only the second that gives man the right to "use all means we can to defend ourselves" (p. 190). He also insists on justice and even equality, "for equal distribution is the law of nature" (p. 213)—though in his view this can only be guaranteed under the coercive autocrat.

Hobbes is often viewed with distaste today, perhaps mainly because a good deal of his analysis is still too near the knuckle for comfort. It is a gloomy thought that the doctrine of "protection" in exchange for what is effectively a partial surrender of natural rights is still proving more effective in keeping the peace than the ethically more attractive but impotent and inadequately binding international "social contract" of the United Nations, in which nothing is surrendered and where all enjoy a purely theoretical equality. None of this is a reason for resigning ourselves to "reality"; but any attempt to improve things must start from a recognition of the real position in world affairs, and many parts of the world have not progressed far beyond Hobbes.

Hobbes has a number of attractions for contemporary Anglo-Saxon politicians: His scientific materialism, the empiricism of his theory of knowledge, and his weak view of human freedom are some of the basic constituents of our "common sense." It is no doubt for this reason that his writings are still an occasional quarry for British and American statesmen seeking historical or philosophical dispensation for tough policies—on those occasions when philosophers are quoted in their speeches.

Many would find Niccolò Machiavelli even more worthy of quotation but might hesitate, for obvious reasons, to invoke his name. Nevertheless, he was first and foremost a diplomat. He was also a very successful diplomat, though even Aristotle would not suggest that he had acquired virtue by the practice of his functions. Yet like Hobbes, Machiavelli improves on closer acquaintance. His theories are not an incitement to evil but a prudent reaction to the violent uncertainties of the world he lived in and specifically to the very real external threat to his native Florence. Machiavelli had seen the consequences of inadequate, vacillating leadership and was especially scathing about the "lax, credulous" Holy Roman Emperor Maximilian I ("The Art of War" in Machiavelli: *The Chief Works and Others,* p. 1098). By causing confusion, weak leadership made diplomacy difficult and peace hard to sustain.

A good deal of Machiavelli's cynicism was skin-deep. In the circumstances of the time, it was perfectly reasonable to warn that if "a prince insists on making it his business to be good among so many people who are not, he will destroy not only himself but others with him" *(The Prince,* p. 58). However reprehensible his methods, it is not possible to argue that Machiavelli's motives were always unworthy. The word he chose to epitomize the cardinal quality needed by effective rulers, *virtù,* is the clue to his approach to ethics, as to other aspects of his thought.

Virtù needs careful translation. It is closer to "virtuosity" than to "virtue," to ability rather than moral worth. This may seem to suggest that unscrupulous cleverness is set above all moral considerations. But it reflects not so much systematized immorality as ingenuity or brilliant opportunism in defense of one's state or in the maintenance of the balance of power. Machiavelli himself at one point defines *virtù* as "a mind ready to turn in any direction as fortune's winds and the variability of affairs require" *(The Prince,* p. 66).

It is important to remember that *virtù* was to be used in the service of something not too far removed from what we would call self-determination. To put things in a purely twentieth-century context, it is of interest to ask ourselves how we would judge a Machiavelli in charge of the diplomacy of a present-day emerging African or Middle Eastern state. Competence alone cannot claim to bring its own moral justification. But the plain truth is that Machiavelli was good at diplomacy, and many of his instinctive critics would be far more sympathetic towards him if he were reincarnated as a modern-day champion of Third World self-determination: As a Gamal Nasser or a Julius Nyerere.

Looked at dispassionately, the supreme cynic was guilty less of immorality than of excess in the Aristotelian sense. His famous injunctions to guile and deceit in diplomacy were not the result of an instinct for deception but the lessons of experience. He simply failed Aristotle's lucid test of the golden mean: He was immoral not because he was evil but because he went too far.

He lived, of course, in extravagant times of almost unhealthy refinement, even in art. Just as the Venetian painters of the day were carried away by the brilliance of their own techniques to the point of endangering the structure of their works, so Machiavelli was dazzled by his own virtuosity in deceit, in defense of the otherwise laudable aim of freeing Italy from French and Spanish incursions.

Machiavelli would be surprised to find how literally some commentators read his writings. His cynicism was not unselfconscious. It was a reflection of his "virtuosity"—as when he castigated Cesare Borgia (whose ruthlessness he otherwise admired) for supposing that the words of another were any more to be relied on than his own.

Machiavelli must have known that his words to Borgia, taken seriously and strictly observed, must preclude diplomacy in any meaningful sense and can only logically lead to perpetual warfare. His view that a prince would make little progress if he were the only white sheep in a black flock cannot be taken to its logical extreme either, simply on the analogy of honor among thieves. Even in the worst of all possible worlds, systematized cynicism is not a workable policy. Machiavelli would have read and noted Socrates' observation in *The Republic:* "But I am wondering whether a state can do without justice when it is asserting its superior powers over another . . ." *(Ethical Theories,* p. 41).

There are other reasons to suppose that he would have understood this message perfectly well. Machiavelli combined a passion for ingenuity in statesmanship with a passionate devotion to liberty. *The Prince* shows one side of him, *The Discourses* another. In the latter he makes it clear that ingenuity is not to be used exclusively in the service of absolutism but in the preservation of individual freedom, and he describes his typically intricate system of checks and balances to secure and maintain this freedom.

All this is powerful fuel for today's debates. Modern-day "realists" might conclude, for example, that the West could do with a little more guile, even ruthlessness, when dealing with powers dedicated to the destruction of democracies. They might point to the inhibitions placed on the work of the covert intelligence services by freedom of information acts and quote Machiavelli's warning that "it is impossible for a republic to succeed in standing still and enjoying its liberties, simply because of the tides of international political life" (The Discourses, p. 379). It is true that Machiavelli saw clearly the impact of the ebb and flow of international affairs on the internal stability of states, and his doctrine that liberty at home can only be firmly secured by an active foreign policy is in itself a powerful argument against isolationism. The Pietist's riposte might be that, in a democratic state, Machiavelli's devotion to liberty might lead him to restrain the executive in both its internal and external functions. In other words, as a modern "prince," he might be tempted by an arms for hostages exchange with Iran, but constrained by the democratic doctrines he would be obliged, in the twentieth century, to uphold.

Writing in England in the sixteenth century, Francis Bacon praised Machiavelli for describing "what men do, and not what they ought to do." Stripped of the layers of caricature with which they have become encrusted, Machiavelli's writings are the most intelligent exposé of the Brutalist tradition. They cannot be ignored, if only because—as in the case of Hobbes—we still recognize all too easily the world they describe.

Utilitarianism, as a moral doctrine, may sound more obviously in tune with our own times. Yet this quintessentially nineteenth-century approach to ethics is beginning to show its age sooner than the thinking of Hobbes, Machiavelli, or Kant. The notion that the morality of an action can be assessed by how far it promotes the greatest quantity of pleasure for the greatest number reflects every sort of Victorian prejudice—above all, the belief in quantifiable facts. Even though the theory was not closely linked to foreign policy by Jeremy Bentham or John Stuart Mill, its chief proponents, its importance in this field has been well recognized since.

One of the main difficulties with utilitarianism—recognized at the time—is that of devising a means whereby the "good"—pleasure or happiness—could be scientifically measured. Bentham developed a scale against which to calibrate the results of an action, using as yardsticks intensity, duration, certainty, propinquity, fecundity, purity, and extent. It is hard enough to see how such categories could be applied as a sociological tool; to use them to estimate the "greatest good" likely to flow from a particular action for the largest number of countries would be entertaining indeed.

To take a particular act of foreign policy: A war could in the end add to the sum total of human happiness because of the years of peace that may ensue once a troublesome tyrant is invaded and overthrown. To justify this view by the use of Bentham's scale would involve some interesting cross-cultural judgments. If one of the countries were China, to begin with, we would need a differential calculus to take care of the length of China's civilization; against the span of her history the, say, twenty years of peace that could follow war might seem like a momentary interlude and would presumably be felt as such by some of her population—though China would gain in numbers what it lost in duration and per capita intensity of peaceful pleasure!

Utilitarianism is thought by many to be a faulty principle. It is certainly an inadequate one. As a measure of the morality or otherwise of an action, it needs to be complemented by greater emphasis on motives and means and less on consequences. Yet there are occasions when the utilitarian calculus seems to be a helpful part of the moral argument. In the running debate on the ethics of nuclear weapons one of the most familiar claims is that, however obnoxious the notion of training weapons of mass destruction on others, it works: Without nuclear weapons, the argument goes, we would never have enjoyed over forty years peace in Europe after World War II.

Whatever one thinks of that proposition, it is a nice illustration both of the strengths and weaknesses of the Benthamite method. It is surely true that the balance of nuclear terror has induced healthy prudence and that untold millions may have benefited from the absence of either conventional or nuclear war. But as soon as too much weight is attached to this single factor or to the numbers of years peace per individual, a small voice inside us objects: First to the means by which this peace is obtained—over-reliance on nuclear weapons—and next to the implicit suggestion that we are living from year to year. "So far, so good" is never a very comforting maxim, especially in nuclear matters.

Bentham's calculations were underpinned by the Victorian belief in linear progress and in the onward march of enlightened citizenry. In Europe alone, two world wars have shaken that belief, even if they have not destroyed it. Neither our statesmen nor our citizens have shown themselves to be as enlightened as the Victorians hoped. Those who argue that nuclear weapons have given us the longest period of peace in this century are using the Benthamite arithmetic while rejecting one of the main assumptions underlying it; they share his mathematical consequentialism, but not his implicit optimism about human nature. Thus perhaps the most profound objection to utilitarianism is its assumption that people do in fact desire the "general happiness" at all. As Henry Sidgewick, an "intuitional utilitarian," pointed out in his *The Methods of Ethics*, this is not necessarily so: An aggregate of the actual desires of the majority may not add up to the required sum. If this is indeed the case in civil society, it seems at least as uncertain that the collectivity of states can automatically be relied upon to aspire to the good of all and to act accordingly.

The paradox of utilitarianism is that although it is meant to be a robustly practical doctrine, on closer scrutiny it can dissolve into the ether, as Thomas Macaulay once showed:

> *The principle of Mr. Bentham, if we understand it, is this, that mankind ought to act so as to produce the greatest happiness. The word* ought, *he tells us, has no meaning, unless it be used with reference to some interest. But the interest of a man is synonymous with his greatest happiness; and therefore to say that a man ought to do a thing, is to say that it is for his greatest happiness to do it. And to say that mankind* ought *to act so as to produce their greatest happiness, is to say that the greatest happiness is the greatest happiness—and that is all!* ("Defence of Mill," Miscellaneous Writings, p. 162)

The caustic Macaulay was being a little unfair; but his unfairness no doubt procured him no little happiness.

Utilitarianism has come under increasing attack over another flaw in the theory—one that Mill himself foresaw and tried to deal with. This is the objection that by coldly and mechanically assessing consequences to the exclusion of motivation and by counting "happy heads" as our main criterion in assessing the morality of an action, we are neglecting both the rights of individuals and minorities and disregarding our wider humanitarian duties. Mill was admitting the problem when he recognized in *Utilitarianism* that some utilitarians cultivated their moral feelings, but not their sympathies. In the last resort, however, he was thrown back on the position that individual happiness would be taken care of by the majority's desire for the good of all—which takes us back to Sidgewick's objection and eventually again to Macaulay.

In foreign policy the immediate attractions of utilitarianism as a rule of thumb need no elaboration. In today's terms the invasion of Grenada is as close as we are likely to get to a live model—though a single illustration does not prove a theory that is faulty on many other grounds. Here is a case where the doctrine could be applied almost neat and where even Bentham's calculus could be persuasive. In a country the size of Grenada it would almost be possible to measure the extent, the likely duration, and even the intensity of the islanders' reaction to the American invasion or liberation. The overwhelming majority like it and feel more secure as a result. This does not dispose of the more complex objections of principle, but it is at least a quantitative defense of America's action. It could even be argued with Mill that the happiness of the minority, who did not at first like the invasion, was subsumed in the general welcome—a way of saying that the minority too would ultimately benefit from the restoration of democracy and that doubts about American motives or means are thus trivial by comparison. The same could not be argued of the Falklands operation by the British, which cost 250 British and more enemy lives to preserve the right to self-determination of 1800 inhabitants. Unless the pleasures of self-determination are more intense than usually supposed, the griefs and deaths would outweigh them—not to speak of financial calculations. The two examples of Grenada and the Falklands ignore a whole range of other factors such as the meaning of sovereignty in their very different situations. They show only that utilitarianism can occasionally have an easy appeal, but that it is a rough and ready and highly fallible moral gauge, even in its own terms.

Vietnam, human rights, and Third World problems

have combined to give the debate about utilitarianism a new importance. In their search for moral laws that will dilute the element of cold calculation and political expediency and give greater prominence to the ethical ghost in the machine, critics of utilitarianism have tended to look back to Kant.

Unlike both utilitarians and Hobbes, Kant believed that citizens and states should co-operate on grounds of duty as well as prudence. In his *Critique of Pure Reason,* he argued that although "our knowledge begins with experience, it does not follow that it arises from experience." In other words there are other considerations to be taken into account. In ethics these are the categorical imperatives.

Kant is the perfect foil for the worldly wise "professionals": At one and the same time he was a man of remarkably sane judgment and a passionate believer in the freedom of the press; a man who never travelled but who talked excellent sense on international affairs; an "idealist" who insisted on the congruity of practice and theory; and a writer of legendary opacity, whose thoughts seemed sometimes shrouded in transcendental vapor, yet one who drew up a model "peace treaty" between states of crystalline clarity.

For Kant moral goodness was to be found not in actions or consequences but in the will when it acted out of duty in accord with the commands of reason: One can be good if one wants to. Morality is above all an achievement of the free use of the rational will. His "categorical imperative" applies as obviously to states as to individual citizens: "Act only according to a maxim by which you can at the same time will that it shall become a universal law" *(Foundations of the Metaphysics of Morals,* p. 339).

Kant was among the few philosophers who wrote specifically on international affairs, and he saw more clearly than others the link between domestic policy and peace among nations. Although he wavered between support for enlightened monarchs, like Frederick the Great, and more democratic forms of government, there is no doubt that he was by inclination what we would loosely call a democrat ("republican" in his contemporary terminology).

He understood before others that the same instinctive "unsociability" that causes men to band together in civil societies within their own countries for each other's protection is necessary abroad too; otherwise, internally "protected peoples" will merely go to war with each other. Unlike Hobbes, who concluded that coercive leadership was necessary to preserve liberty, Kant's recipe was a league of nations, which would give justice and security to even the smallest of its members *(Idea for a Universal History,* p. 11).

None of the pessimistic overtones of Hobbes clouds his approach. In Kant's estimation states do learn by experience; to that extent he is a believer in progress, saying that "after many reformative revolutions, a universal cosmopolitan condition, which nature has as her ultimate purpose, will come into being as the womb wherein all the original capacities of the human race can develop" *(Idea for a Universal History,* p. 23). But he insists that progress can only be maintained by the "united will" of nations and peoples.

His famous draft international treaty "Perpetual Peace" (originally published in 1795) is based on the view that international law must be founded on a federation of free states. It is a remarkably enlightened document. "No treaty of peace shall be held valid in which there is tacitly reserved matter for a future war," it asserts *(Perpetual Peace,* p. 3). "No independent states, whether large or small, shall come under the dominion of another state by inheritance, exchange, purchase or donation" (p. 4). Acts of hostility that would make mutual confidence in peace impossible (e.g., espionage) are also banned, as are military pressures: "No state shall interfere by force with the constitutional government of another state" (p. 7); and "Standing armies shall in time be totally abolished" (p. 5).

Kant was concerned lest a credit system that grew beyond bounds should give rise to a dangerous moneyed power, constituting an inexhaustible war chest and so be a threat to peace. This was what he had in mind when he said in his draft peace treaty: "National debts shall not be contracted with a view to the external friction of states" (p. 6). The emphasis on the expensiveness and danger of standing armies is also elaborated in *Idea for a Universal History*. In a passage that sums up the key elements of his political thinking, he draws together the questions of ethics, education, and war:

> *So long as states waste their forces in vain and violent self-expansion, thereby constantly thwarting the slow efforts to improve the minds of those citizens by even withdrawing all support from them, nothing in the way of a moral order is to be expected. For such an end a long internal working of each political body towards the education of its citizens is required* (Idea for a Universal History, *p. 21*).

There would be little difficulty in illustrating the point today, whether by belligerence in the impoverished Third World or by the difficulty of balancing social against defense budgets in the West.

Many of the principles enunciated by Kant are enshrined in the United Nations Charter today. But in a sense Kant was in advance of the Charter. He understood that international cooperation is not just a matter of laying down fine principles: Democratic government is a precondition for real security among states, and democratic government in turn depends on a free press, and above all a higher degree of public enlightenment.

Kant's "perpetual peace" is not high-minded theory; it is full of remarkably shrewd and sensible insights—insights on commerce—"the spirit of commerce, which is incompatible with war, sooner or later takes the upper hand in every state" *(Perpetual Peace,* p. 32); on the duties of the media in promoting democracy through enlightenment; on the importance of open government and the risks of secret diplomacy; and even on what we would now call freedom of movement among countries—"universal hospitality" *(Perpetual Peace,* p. 20) in Kant's imaginative phrase.

But for the modern world perhaps the most intriguing aspects of his work are those that foreshadow the achievement of the United States and the European Economic Community (EEC):

> *The practicability (objective reality) of this idea of federation, which should gradually spread to all states and thus lead to perpetual peace, can be proved. For as fortune directs that a powerful and enlightened people can make itself a republic, which by its nature must be inclined to perpetual peace, this gives a fulcrum to the federation of other states so that they adhere to it and thus secure freedom under the idea of the law of nations. By more and more such associations, the federation may be gradually extended* (Perpetual Peace, *p. 18*).

The EEC still falls short of the philosopher's idea in a number of ways. The main limitation is the community's regional rather than global ethos: It does not see itself as a nucleus of a universal "federation of free states" *(Perpetual Peace,* p. 16). But in other respects the community incarnates the spirit and even occasionally the letter of his thinking, which was influenced by an optimistic view of developments in France at the time. The EEC emerged after centuries of vicious warfare and only after the establishment of true democracies in all the countries concerned. The process of gradual accretion, recommended by Kant, has continued since its foundation in almost exactly the way he described, with Spain and Greece joining after the return of each country to representative government.

The original form of the community is unashamedly economic, its founders believing, like Kant, that the "spirit of commerce is incompatible with war." Although it is true that European armies are still standing, it seems unlikely that Kant was sufficiently unworldly to suggest that the democracies should disarm while still waiting for other countries (now, those of Eastern Europe) to embark on the road to representative government.

On military questions as a whole, Kant's thinking is often uncannily relevant to modern preoccupations. His concept of "humanity as an end in itself" *(Foundations of the Metaphysics of Morals,* p. 345), with its subordination of immediate political goals to fundamental imperatives, recalls the overriding duty of governments to avoid any action that could precipitate the risk of nuclear conflict. Kant's ethics could also be construed as a powerful incentive to arms control and disarmament. Although the point is admittedly anachronistic, in response to the utilitarian view that the present balance works, should be allowed to continue, and perhaps should even be refined, Kant might have argued that it is the rational moral duty of states constantly to strive to bring the level of armaments down and seek ways to dispense altogether with nuclear weapons, which threaten "humanity as an end in itself." Given his conviction that peace must be based on education as well as freedom, he might even have suggested that any eventual financial savings might be applied to recruiting more competent school teachers.

Travelling back in time through the unhealthy miasmas of German romantic idealism, with its apotheosis of the state, to the more humane visions of Kant can be like groping one's way back to sanity, and to a certain hope. But in the last resort, if only because of the nuclear incubus of the late twentieth century, it is hard to share entirely the optimism about the moral progress of mankind that Kant himself sustained in old age, despite the atrocities of the French Revolution. He discovered an *a priori* predisposition to progress in the fact of human hope itself: Hope is a presupposition of action, a postulate of practical reason. To a modern layman, the difficulty here is that hopelessness could easily take root *a priori* in the soil of today's moral despair. It depends where you start from.

But Kant would have had an answer. One of his fiercest injunctions is against the temptation to derive moral principles from particular circumstances or traits of human character and thereby sacrifice the principle of universality. In *Foundations of the Metaphysics of Morals* he attacked those who attempt to find ethical guidelines in "contingent grounds," which in his view "substitute for morality a bastard patched up from limbs of very different parentage, which looks like anything one wishes to see in it, but not like virtue to anyone who has ever beheld her in her true form" (p. 343).

Contemporary philosophers of public affairs are clearly under far greater pressure than Kant himself in the eighteenth century to do just that: To develop ethical principles on the basis of a purely political conjuncture or of a particular party's program. Some would argue that today's "universality" is ensured by the media. But even if this argument is accepted, it is purchased at the price of historical perspective. What is won in space is lost in time. Nothing would be easier than to construct a whole system of domestic political ethics around the Watergate affair or of international morality around the Vietnam war. Whether Kant could have developed his ideas in our international "global village" as fruitfully as he did in his small German town is an intriguing speculation.

There is no obvious equivalent to Kant in our time and certainly no one of his stature who has covered questions of international ethics as comprehensively as he did. We have instead a proliferation of researches into this or that narrow aspect of the debate, as well as some excellent literature by foreign policy experts. Rather than dwell on the specialist work in the field, it would be more in keeping with the overall approach of this chapter to look briefly at the incidence on the ethics of foreign affairs of two major contemporary American philosophers—John Rawls and Willard Van Orman Quine, both of whom reflect and condition the intellectual spirit of the times in different ways.

The scope and popularity of Rawls's *A Theory of Justice* alone brings him into the arena of this discussion. Rawls places himself firmly in the "social contract" tradition of Locke, Rousseau, and Kant. He uses certain simplifying devices to bring out the full force of this line of thinking. One is his invention of something called "the original position" (*A Theory of Justice*, p. 12)—a state of equality corresponding to the state of nature in the traditional social contract theory, which was begun by Hobbes (about whom he has reservations). He is careful to emphasize that such a position could never actually have existed: It is a purely hypothetical construct to ease understanding. The central idea is that in this "original position" everybody operates behind a "veil of ignorance" about his place in society, natural abilities, intelligence, strength, or moral disposition. It is behind this "veil" that principles of justice would be elaborated.

In these circumstances, Rawls believes that ordinary rational people would come to two central conclusions. First, each person would wish to have an equal right to the most extensive basic liberty compatible with a similar liberty for others. Second, social and economic equalities would be arranged so that they were both a) reasonably expected to be to everyone's advantage and b) attached to positions and offices open to all.

There are evident possibilities of extending these principles to relations among states. Disappointingly, Rawls has so far made only the briefest attempt to do so.

In one sense, this reticence seems healthy: A coherent system of civil justice at home should presumably precede any attempt at internationalization. Kant would have approved of the priorities, and in his 1985 lecture, "Justice as Fairness: Political not Metaphysical," Rawls agrees that his theory presupposes a particular type of democratic society. But this is not admitted in "A Theory of Justice," and the temptation to substitute countries for the individuals who meet, notionally, in this "original position" to elaborate principles of justice at the beginning of time is irresistible. And if we believe in the essential unity of the moral behavior of countries and individuals, states and statesmen, any flaws in the theory will be highlighted as much by its international as its domestic application.

It may seem vulgar to drag Rawls's highly abstract construction down to the level of the everyday. But we start from where we are, not in limbo behind a curtain. The notion of reasonable men meeting in private to reach reasonable solutions, unaware of their relative positions and strengths, is particularly unfortunate in the case of diplomacy. It is an image that is too close to the grinding reality of routine practice to serve as a convincing metaphor: The collision of theory with that reality is instantaneous and painful. As it happens, one of the principal tasks of diplomacy is precisely to get the right people into a room together at the right place and time—that is, when circumstances are most conducive to agreement. It is almost equally important to keep ill-intentioned or unrepresentative people out. That, basically, is what all the difficulty in securing solutions in Afghanistan or the Middle East has been about.

Even assuming that they can be coaxed into the room, the supposedly reasonable people will in fact insist on sitting in a configuration that reflects the existing power and prestige of their countries or current alliances, thus to some extent preempting the discussion. They may also insist on speaking their own languages, which will influence the negotiations in a number of practical or symbolic ways. All this leaves aside social background, temperament, and national characteristics—which is leaving aside a great deal. But enough has been said to make it clear that it is often exceedingly difficult to agree on the format of such meetings or even on an agenda for discussion. It is a truism of diplomacy that a successful conference or summit meeting is one that has been "properly prepared." This often means prenegotiations through trusted emissaries or private deals in the corridors. In other words, the meeting itself is likely either to be a failure or something of a formality, assuming it can be engineered at all.

The fact is that foreign policy is permanently in the "original position," but in more of a Hobbesian and Kantian than a Rawlsian sense. In effect, Hobbes was suggesting that international contracts are necessary to save countries from their own worst instincts, in the same way that the social contract is necessary at home. Kant, though more optimistic, also believed that the state of nature would linger on in international affairs, even after more civilized commonwealths were established in each country. In their different ways, each of these models is persuasive. But when Rawls touches briefly on foreign affairs, he is far less convincing, and we are alerted to certain questionable presuppositions about human nature on which his wider theory is based.

In his brief attempt to reconstitute the "social contract" in an international context, Rawls himself places representatives of nations in the same "original position" as individuals and assumes they are deprived of various kinds of information; isolated, as it were, both from their foreign ministries and their national histories. He assumes that in such a framework agreement on the equality of nations would be easily reached, as would the right of a people to settle their own affairs without the intervention of foreign powers, and the right of self-defense, including the formation of alliances for this purpose. He then suggests that these principles could be used to define when a nation has a just cause of war.

This argument begs a number of crucial questions. In real life, the first problem that the national representatives would have to ponder is what constitutes a "people"; without that, self-determination would be meaningless—vide the Palestinians. If it were simply a matter of fair-minded people acknowledging the principle, then Rawls is behind events: It is already inscribed in the United Nations Charter, along with many other worthy sentiments. To that extent, a meeting in the "original position" has already taken place—in San Francisco in 1945. The charter was signed by many countries, including the Soviet Union through its representative Vyacheslav Molotov, whose attachment to the principle of self-determination can reasonably be questioned. (The same hand that signed the charter signed Stalin's death lists too, adding obscene comments against some of the names.)

This objection—that real-life diplomacy is a tortuous business—does not wholly invalidate the Rawlsian approach. But at best, Rawls is telling us something that Kant already knew: Like-minded societies would find little fundamental difficulty in agreeing on the fundamental principles of international co-operation. On any serious interpretation of the term there are only about twenty to thirty working democracies in the world at present, out of about 160 members of the United Nations. Most of these countries would sign up cheerfully enough to Rawls's principles, as Molotov did in the case of the U.N. Charter, in the full knowledge that he would come under no domestic democratic pressure to implement them.

The second principle elaborated behind the veil of ignorance, which holds that any inequalities must be to everyone's advantage, could be extended more fruitfully to the foreign field. To begin with, it recognizes the inevitability of inequality among nations. Clearly the size, geographical position, population, and national resources of a country are far greater inhibitions to the "upward mobility" of a state than the equivalent circumstances of an individual. But the essential element of Rawls's formula—that inequalities cannot be static if they are to be justified—is the same; there must be scope for the relative improvement of the position of each country if it is to be brought to accept the principle.

In the real world this means an enlightened policy on aid and trade by the larger powers towards the smaller and weaker, as well as the necessity of the larger powers' refraining from any interference with smaller countries' security or internal affairs. That in turn requires that such societies should be sufficiently altruistic to make the necessary financial sacrifices—which takes us straight back to Kant's emphasis on an enlightened public opinion.

In the late twentieth century, we tend to think of ourselves as more scientific thinkers than our predecessors. And yet Rawls's overall approach has a curiously ethereal, almost dreamy quality when compared to that of Kant, who seems more firmly grounded in reality. The meeting of representatives in the "original position" is an eye-catching innovation; but even among the apostles, one failed to live up to the mark.

There is an assumption—admitted in part by Rawls himself—that a sort of intellectual harmony would emerge from the meeting of representatives in the "original position" without an ethical struggle within each individual or between contending views. His is a morality not of austere command, as in Kant, but of "mutual respect and self-esteem" *(Theory of Justice,* p. 178). There is a bloodless abstraction about all this, an intellectual pietism from which any sense of the tragic in human affairs is curiously missing. Against Rawls's faith in the results of the meeting of pure minds, it is worth counterposing an observation by the German philosopher Martin Heidegger in his letter to Jean-Paul Sartre "On Humanism," where he responds to Sartre's 1946 speech "Existentialism is a Humanism" and takes issue with the idea that any form of international (or for that matter community) activity is good for its own sake: "Nationalism is not overcome through mere internationalism. It is rather expanded and elevated thereby into a system. Nationalism is as little brought and raised to *humanitas* by internationalism as individualism is by an unhistorical collectivism" *(Basic Writings,* p. 221). In a word, there is a whiff of impracticality and therefore of moralism about Rawls's theories: Worthy, elevated moralism, but moralism all the same.

Quine's work is even further removed from the direct field of the ethics of foreign policy than that of Rawls. Yet because of his stature as a philosopher and the sheer scope of his inquiry, we naturally look to him for clues to our current condition in this, as in other fields. Quine has written very little on ethics, but in a sense his theory of meaning subsumes morality. It is spelled out most clearly in his essay "Two Dogmas of Empiricism," where his main conclusion is:

> *The totality of our so-called knowledge or beliefs, from the most casual matters of geography and history to the profoundest laws on atomic physics, or even of pure mathematics and logic, is a man-made fabric, which impinges on experience only along the edges . . .*

> *A conflict with experience on the periphery occasions re-adjustments in the interior of the field . . . but the total field is so undetermined by its boundary conditions, experience, that there is much latitude of choice as to what statements to re-evaluate in the light of any single contrary experience* (From a Logical Point of View, p. 42).

This is a statement about the tentative nature of our relationship to reality. It is a view about the nature of facts rather than of values. But in moral terms, the implications are important. It suggests that the world is "pre-positioned" around us in a "man-made fabric," yet remains difficult for us to define since we respond only sluggishly to the new facts of experience. Applied to foreign policy, it could be contended that this view is highly conservative, reinforcing the belief of an individual country in its position in the world or in its "destiny"—and maybe its illusions—and making it more resistant to any new moral challenge. To this extent, it is a comforting message to practicing politicians and statesmen—comforting to the point of inducing complacency perhaps, recalling as it does the words of Lord Salisbury, the British Foreign Secretary, who once described British foreign policy as drifting lazily downstream, occasionally putting out an oar to avoid a collision.

The main objection to seeing the ethics of foreign policy in these terms is precisely the risk of conservative drift—ethical drift—of policy without direction or clearly defined moral content. At the same time the imagery used by Quine—who concludes that meaning can only take the form of a plaited quilt whose borders form a rough and subjectively defined context—is seductive to anyone operating among the uncertainties of international affairs and who finds himself constantly scanning the shifting fabric of events for significant patterns. The desire to read his own pattern into these events will often predominate. So will the instinct to blur the context in which he is operating even further in order to allow himself the maximum possible latitude.

Judging by his only published work on morality, "On the Nature of Moral Values," it seems that Quine is aware of these dangers. He puts forward the idea of causal reduction to resolve moral conflict. The idea is that when disputes occur, their elements should be refined down to basic moral values that command agreement; and that there must remain some ultimate ends, irreducible and so unjustifiable. This seems to recall the doctrine of the categorical imperative and even in a sense some of Rawls's assumptions, and so gives some shape to the otherwise invertebrate mobility of moral context implied in "Two Dogmas of Empiricism." But unlike Kant, who was straining towards a *possible* consensus, Quine rests his case on an *actual* consensus. Moreover, the emphasis remains heavily on the inevitability of uncertainty and on the difficulty of defining moral meaning or indeed any meaning at all.

Quine's work is clearly far deeper and more diverse than is suggested here. But to a practitioner of foreign policy, conscious of the fluidity that characterizes international relations, what leaps from some of his pages is the stress on the blurred, ragged edges of "reality." The fundamental task of establishing precisely what the motivations and intentions of a potential adversary or even a friend are or what the foreign policy of either *means* is frequently underestimated by most critics of international affairs, even though one's own assessment of the aims of the opponent and how legitimate these may be will be a central factor in conditioning the morality or otherwise of one's own response. The unnatural stiffness and formalism of diplomatic intercourse reflects a more or less conscious effort to give shape and significance to the anarchic underside of international relationships. There could be no better practical illustration of this aspect of foreign affairs than Quine's doctrine of unavoidable imprecision.

A possible objection to this view is that we are increasingly better equipped by modern technology to establish the truth about the intentions of others. But a moment's reflection on the idea that improved communications make us better informed, thereby giving us a more precise context to work in, shows that it is a momentous fallacy. It is certainly the case that more facts may be transmitted more quickly and more securely; but the problem of selection and interpretation grows geometrically with the amount of information available, and with it the possibilities of reading arbitrary significance into isolated "facts" or tangled mounds of raw intelligence.

Fear, suspicion, or malign purpose can influence the way in which such "facts" are collected or impel the analyst to draw selectively on them, inducing unwarranted certainties from intrinsically uncertain situations. If anyone doubts the relevance of such considerations to the practical exigencies of diplomacy and to considerations of morality, it is sufficient to recall that the Korean Airline KAL 007 was flying along the "boundary conditions" of meaning, on the very edge of Quine's plaited quilt. The abundance of electronic information on either side did not prevent its destruction.

Quine's work contains a colorful illustration of the difficulty of interpreting facts. It can be read as a parable by anyone actively concerned with the formation or execution of foreign policy. In his essay "Speaking of Objects," he imagines the situation of a newly discovered tribe whose language is without known affinities. A linguist is therefore obliged to learn the language by observation. This might seem easy enough: When a rabbit appears, for example, he will note that the tribesman makes a certain noise. But as Quine points out, even when a native makes a noise only when a rabbit appears, it by no means follows that the noise means "rabbit." Theoretically at least, it is perfectly possible that he will be referring to some "undetached rabbit part"! Scanners of the press of a foreign country or of the radar screen will immediately see the point of the story.

When it is remembered that statesmen have to decide not only whether to cry "rabbit" on the basis of tentative or tendentious information (or because they themselves may have a predisposition to see rabbits where others do not) but also whether to shoot, capture, or caress the animal (assuming it is there at all) the point becomes less academic and diverting than it may seem at first sight. In terms of threats to national security, real or imagined, the parable becomes very serious indeed.

Quine's cautions on the question of meaning are another reminder of the tenuousness of our moral judgments, which must be based on certifiable "fact" as well as on value. The lesson applies not only to our own day. It might even be suggested that, projected backwards in time, it is an additional warning against automatically extrapolating forward the ethical attitudes of a particular historical context and transferring them to our own conditions when their "meaning" may be still further attenuated. It can be contended that the whole of history itself is presumably a loosely "plaited quilt" too, with its rough edges and inscrutable defining circumstances. With all these caveats in mind, it can still be instructive to test the moral philosophies of previous generations against our current preoccupations to see whether and how the pattern of beliefs and practice of many centuries alters when subjected to the pull of our own experience.

4

THE
MORAL
CONTINUUM

*There cannot be any Progress
(true progress, that is to say
moral) except within the
individual and by the individual
himself.*
—*BAUDELAIRE*, Intimate Journals

▼

Moral behavior cannot be neatly segmented into public and private spheres. Statesmen do not function on some alternative ethical current, while the rest of us are on D.C. The notion that individual and public behavior are part of a moral continuum seems so obvious as to defy proof—like arguing the unity of the elements. Yet a good deal of what is written about ethics and public affairs both from the Pietist and Brutalist angles is based on the opposite assumption.

Examples are manifold, but Stuart Hampshire, a distinguished contemporary British moral philosopher, provides us inadvertently with the perfect illustration of the point. In his essay "Morality and Pessimism," which forms part of a collection on the subject of public and private morality, he argues, perfectly reasonably, that those in public life bear an added burden of responsibility. That seems clear enough, and Hampshire justifies his thesis in a number of ways.

He sees the most obvious reasons for this differentiation in the greater and more enduring consequences of public acts. This is part and parcel of representing the interests of the electorate in a democratic state. Although Hampshire does not say so, it is important to note that these are differences in degree and not in kind. It is on this crucial point of difference in kind that he seems to carry the argument too far. His essay is an implied indictment of the American government, written in the aftermath of the Vietnam war. This aim colors the argument and leads him to a highly revealing *excès de zèle*, which acts as a warning signal to the reader that the argument is switching from the philosophical to the political plane. The passage itself sounds innocuous enough: "Lowering the barriers of prohibition, and making rational calculation of consequence the sole foundation of public policies, have so far favoured and are still favouring a new callousness of policy, a dullness of sensibility and sometimes moral despair, *at least in respect of public affairs*" (italics added; "Morality and Pessimism," p. 16). The implication is that the United States showed an extreme degree of moral ruthlessness in using its technological superiority to prosecute the war in Vietnam. As a comment on that war, Hampshire's observation is widely shared by European and indeed current American opinion—but minus the last phrase, which distinguishes between private and public behavior. Yet this phrase invalidates the whole sentence. The author is not merely saying that the American government behaved badly; he is implying that there are two separate, ethical worlds, one reflecting the moral aspirations of individuals and the other the impious activities of governments or their agents.

That is a comfortable doctrine for liberal-minded academics, for critics of foreign policy, and indeed for the public itself; but it is a false one. The importance of Hampshire's remark is that it encapsulates a form of moral escapism with regard to public affairs that, though honorable enough in its motivations, can have a highly damaging effect on ethical thinking. His statement is misleading in a very important way. It implies a dislocation between personal and state morality, as if the two were different spheres, and ignores the fact that democratic accountability works both ways. Individuals elected the governments who prosecuted the Vietnam war. Imbued as the essay is with the spirit of the times, when the public was dismayed or disgusted by the war, the shaky premises on which such observations were based may have escaped notice. But they seem stark to us now.

The clue is to read the passage not as a comment on foreign policy at all but as one on modern sexual mores, which of course evolved in important ways during exactly the same period in the 1960s when the American engagement in Vietnam was escalating under a series of presidents, including John F. Kennedy. In retrospect, the passage can be read as a poignant and perceptive warning about the consequences of sexual "liberation." What Hampshire is rightly deploring is the utilitarian approach, in which actions are dictated not by ethical considerations but by mere "rational calculation of consequences." But he could be speaking not just of defoliation or the high-level bombing of jungles in Indochina but the moral consequences of abortion and improved birth-control techniques, or the general relaxation of sexual taboos. It is not necessary to be of a crusty or reactionary frame of mind to wonder whether such developments have not "lowered the barriers to prohibition" and stimulated a "new callousness . . . a dullness of sensibility and sometimes moral despair" in many a young life. Nor does one need to be a fanciful Freudian to perceive a very clear parallel between indiscriminate sex and indiscriminate bombing, in ethical terms at least. The scourge of AIDS had not begun when Hampshire wrote, but had his essay in fact been about sex, read retrospectively the passage could be cited as a somber warning against the excesses of the sexual revolution of the sixties.

Read as he wrote it, the whole purpose of the Professor's remarks—to distinguish between some new harshness in public policy, quite disassociated from individual behavior in society as a whole—is instantly undermined when seen in this larger context. It would be risky to press the parallel too far but forgivable to chase it a little further down the track. Is a society where family life is disintegrating and the divorce rate soaring, and where many of the decisions which lead to these developments are based on the sort of amoral utilitarianism Hampshire deplores in Vietnam, more or less likely to improve its international behavior, for example by honoring treaties in the "family of nations"?

The truth about Hampshire's observation is that it is meaningless when narrowly applied to the ethics of public policy, though a wise enough lament on the contemporary human condition as a whole. It tells us nothing that is peculiar to international relations, but a good deal about the Zeitgeist of the 1960s. The worst interpretation would be that it reflects a pernicious political attitude, which allows the moral critic to issue generalized calls for restraint by governments, while preserving the myth of the purity of individual motivation among the governed. This seems an impractical basis for the more ethical conduct of public affairs. In the view of Edmund Burke, the virtues which restrain the appetite are at least nine out of ten of the virtues, and it is no good trying to substitute for this some unspecific appeal to "humanity" or "benevolence." Burke is right because he was talking not just about governments but about human nature as a whole.

Hampshire's essay—though perhaps not typical of his writing—highlights a strain of neo-Rousseauist moral escapism in contemporary studies of the philosophy of public affairs. The burden of ethical responsibility is subtly shifted from individuals onto "society," "the government," or its "agents," who are implicitly portrayed as thwarting the transparently virtuous ethical urges of the people by "hiding the facts," "sheltering behind veils of secrecy," or otherwise manipulating information. As part of this ethical construct, governments are depicted as behaving with a harshness—especially in foreign policy—that is alien to the natural disposition of their electors.

There are deeper waters here, which were brilliantly explored by Irving Babbitt in *Rousseau and Romanticism*. There is a self-evident link between the "temperament" of a people and its foreign policy. If that temperament happens to be of the sentimental variety, chastised by Babbitt, that policy will be inherently unstable. A self-indulgent society—the awful word "permissive" is inescapable—is perhaps more likely to behave impermissibly toward other nations. Mawkish, indulgent, and emotional states of mind are quite compatible with harsh actions towards other countries, as toward other individuals. As Babbitt points out,

> *The triumph of egoism over altruism in the relations between man and man is even more evident in the relations between nation and nation. The egoism that results from the in-breeding of the temperament on a national scale, runs in the case of strong nations into imperialism. We have not reflected sufficiently on the fact that the soft temperamentalist Rousseau is more than any other one person a father of* Kultur . . . (Rousseau and Romanticism, *p. 157*).

(On the individual level, it was Rousseau himself who, while anxious to deliver whole peoples from the chains of tyranny, delivered his own illegitimate children, without scruple, into public care. . . .)

Hampshire is not alone in making a false distinction between private and public morality. Thomas Nagel, one of the leading figures in contemporary American moral philosophy, writes in very much the same vein in "Ruthlessness in Public Life" (the title gives the flavor of the argument), where he states: "The great modern crimes are public crimes. To a degree the same can be said of the past, but the growth of political power has introduced a scale of massacre and despoilation that makes the efforts of private criminals, pirates and bandits seem truly modest" *(Public and Private Morality,* p. 75). Again, the immediate historical background is Vietnam. For anyone not engaged in the same line of essentially political thinking as the author, this passage, while superficially convincing, is in fact highly confusing. The word "public" itself is ambiguous and can be read in at least two ways: Are we talking about crimes carried out by governments with the tacit or openly expressed assent of the electorate—bearing mind that the blame for Vietnam can be spread across a number of presidents, all of whom were democratically elected; or of crimes by individual statesmen, who have somehow succeeded in gaining office while disguising their immoral purpose? Either way, Nagel seems to admit that this does not represent any change historically, since "public crimes" have rarely been wanting. We are told instead that there are more such crimes now than in the past, though even this quantitative distinction is dubious: How many deaths were there in China through wars and subsequent famines?

The argument is not illuminated by the use of the curious phrase "the growth of political power"; it can only be assumed that it refers to the increase in the authority of democratic governments by virtue of their very representativeness, coupled with the improvement of the technology of persuasion, in the form of media exploitation, or the technology of coercion, in the form of modern armies. Whatever the interpretation of the phrase, one would have thought that any such increase in political power would put at least as heavy an ethical burden on the individual voter as on the elected leader, who is in the nature of things expected to express the popular will.

Finally, Nagel's comparison with private enterprise crime effectively explodes the argument. It highlights the fact that criminals on a large or petty scale, together with a vast number of other imperfect citizens, elect or tolerate leaders who, like themselves, are increasingly well-equipped by the march of science to cause multiple injuries to others in pursuit of private or public purpose. Three random examples are noise, bad driving, and the cultural contusion inflicted on millions by the mass media.

Hence, like Hampshire, while claiming to make a crucial distinction between the way we *are* and the way our leaders *act*, Nagel is not in fact saying very much at all. He certainly does not succeed in proving that the modern sovereign's capacity for evil exceeds that of Carlyle's shoeblack (who now elects and controls him). At the very most he is suggesting that the sovereign's responsibilities are weightier—which is undisputed and hardly news.

So far we have concentrated on the excesses of "liberal" attitudes to the ethics of foreign affairs—those of the Pietists. Surface manifestations of this line of thinking may appear very different from those of "conservative," or Brutalist, commentators on foreign policy, but the underlying misapprehensions are the same. In the latter case we are merely dealing with "hard" rather than "soft" sentimentalists (*Rousseau and Romanticism*, p. 157); both are different emanations of romanticism and moral evasion.

In *Law, Morality and War in the Contemporary World* Hans Morgenthau seeks to define the nature of foreign affairs, claiming that "International politics can be defined as a continuing effort to maintain and increase the power of one's nation . . . and to keep in check or reduce the power of other nations." Morgenthau, though a realist, is by no means a full-blown Brutalist, which makes this statement all the more significant. It would be a bold critic who would contest its essential truth—certainly not Polymarchus, who disputes with Socrates in Plato's *Republic,* and with whose view of justice as doing harm to enemies and good to friends it seems to accord nicely. But in fact it suffers from the same fundamental flaw as the position of the more liberal critics cited above. Morgenthau implies by his (perhaps deliberately harsh) formulation of the realities of foreign policy that there is some distinction between the behavior of human kind in its domestic and international environments. Although they approach the question from different angles —Nagel implying that public man is a corrupted version of the conscientious citizen and Morgenthau that in his international manifestation, such ruthlessness is inevitable— the conclusion is similar and equally misleading.

Just as Professor Hampshire's lament on public policy can be extended to private ethics, so Professor Morgenthau's definition of international politics is unenlightening. Exactly the same statement he uses to define the field is manifestly as true of all political parties, businesses, football teams, and most individuals as it is of states. In their different ways, all strive constantly to increase their power and to keep that of others in check.

It is a curious fact that each of these statements— whether by Hampshire, Nagel, or Morgenthau—read together or separately somehow inspires instant confidence. It is worth asking ourselves why? The reason seems to be that in their separate ways they appeal to our unreflecting ethical sensibilities rather than to our ethical reason. Hampshire and Nagel are saying that there is a certain ruthlessness in the conduct of some modern states. Who would gainsay that? Instinctively, we tend to agree, and all can think of an example or two. Just as instinctively, we would like to disassociate ourselves morally from such unpleasantness, to disclaim responsibility and register our disapprobation.

Morgenthau is telling us simply that we live in a harsh world, where it is the duty of the state to behave harshly if its interests and those of its citizens are not to be ridden over roughshod by foreigners. Again, we are inclined to accept this line of thinking too, even if it appears to conflict with the "concerned" approach, though again with the reservation that such conduct may be inevitable among nations but has little to do with our own private moral worlds. That is where Hampshire and Nagel come in and why these contradictory positions can appear reconcilable.

Behind all this there is a moral laziness perfectly natural to all of us—a mild version of what Carlyle, with his uncompromising language, once called "putrescent indolence" (see Babbitt's *Rousseau and Romanticism*, p. 128). He was giving vent at the time to his dislike of Samuel Taylor Coleridge, whom he suspected, along with other romantics, of constructing an incense-flavored smokescreen between himself and his moral obligations to his fellow men and women. In the case of the average citizen's attitudes to foreign policy, the posture is so agreeable and so easily understandable that it becomes easily forgivable. But it is surely not an attitude to be indulged in or encouraged by moral philosophers.

There is nothing new in this *de facto* dissociation of ethical sensibilities. The case for seeing diplomacy as operating in a separate ethical sphere has been explored by writers from Machiavelli to Reinhold Niebuhr and Morgenthau, among others, from different angles and at different historical epochs. Many more have assumed, without reflection, that such a dichotomy exists within the nature of things. Reasoned attempts have been made to justify the dualism, and the main ingredients in the Brutalists' arguments and assumptions seem to be as follows:

a Public policies have greater and therefore more lasting consequences than private actions. They also involve greater responsibilities. Therefore fewer moral scruples are appropriate than in private life. Pursuit of stark self-interest is thus less shocking; indeed, it is a duty. Unselfishness would be a vice. Consequently, the state is entitled to use violence or other unscrupulous actions in defense of its interests in a way that the private individual is not.

b Statesmen need to justify their policies clearly in public. This inevitably involves simplification and a degree of dramatization. They therefore tend to accentuate a single aspect of the argument (e.g., the immediate consequences of an action rather than means and motives as well—hence "one-dimensional" ethics) or otherwise invent a false coherence, which can mask immoral means or ends. More simply, statesmen may lie.

c Collective guilt cannot legally be attached to states or people in the way it is to individuals.

d States have a higher morality that is subsumed in the concept of the destiny of nations.

Not all such claims are necessarily invalid in all instances when applied to foreign policy. But taken as a whole, they all tend to entrench misleading distinctions between private and public ethics. Above all, they imply a deep divide between the moral constraints on equally mortal and fallible men and women, some of whom happen to be involved in diplomacy or politics, others not.

If these assumptions are true, then not only are governments absolved from conventional moral responsibilities for their international acts: The public cannot be held responsible either. The average citizen could claim exemption from

such responsibility on several grounds, but most convincingly by protesting (or affecting) ignorance, having been by
definition debarred from the higher realms in which statesmen conceive and execute their policies: "We were never
told." Alternatively, he could shift the moral incubus by ac-
quiescing actively or tacitly in the proposition that international affairs are a world apart and that the fewer questions
asked, the better.

What we get from all this is in effect a moral vacuum.
The statesman is beyond the reach of conventional morality,
and the public is thereby released from its moral obligations too. Thus we reach the position that while the Pietists
sometimes seem to be saying that only governments have
international moral duties, the Brutalist seems to be suggesting that no one has.

The most familiar arguments for the "ethical apart-
heid" of foreign policy are worth dissecting one by one. The
first—that greater responsibility licenses amorality or immorality or (in the Pietist's view) imposes some more demanding moral code—is disproved by reference to the facts
of everyday life.

An intact family is a microcosm of the international
order. The well-being of its children could be used, by analogy with the "greater responsibility" argument, to legitimize untold misdeeds by parents in charge of their
welfare—misdeeds whose consequences would adversely affect the welfare of other families. Tax evasion and various
routine forms of nepotism—using connections to get a child
a job or into a good school—are two popular examples. Both
states and families habitually behave in selfish ways; when
pressed, each may well attempt to justify such behavior in
terms of higher loyalties. But that alone does not legitimize
the action. Either both states and families, the governors
and the governed, corporations and blood brothers can invoke a "higher moral code," or neither can.

As for the view that the consequences of public acts are

more lasting, what could be more appealing in human terms than the duty of parents to provide for the future of their offspring in order to assure the family (itself an atom of the state) some small measure of immortality? Clearly, in the case of the actions of the state, more people are affected. But it could even be contended—assuming the argument to be worth pursuing—that the statesman has a smaller and not a greater ethical burden. He may have more families in his care but at least his "children" now have the vote, and the responsibilities that go with it.

So we are left not with a hierarchy of ethical values ranging from the great, larger than life "issues" of international affairs to the banal moral dilemmas of everyday existence but with an inextricable amalgam of social and human obligations at home and abroad.

"State violence" is a phrase that would sit as easily on the lips of Machiavelli as on those of a modern left-wing critic—though the first, of course, would see it as a necessary adjunct to diplomacy or government and the second as an abuse of power. But whatever one's view, the idea that the state has a *right* to behave internationally in a way that individuals or societies do not is unpersuasive. The obvious parallel here is between state and civil violence, war abroad and law enforcement at home.

Both national law enforcement agencies and the armed forces are in the same sense under popular control. Theoretically at least, the government and the judiciary can sanction any misdemeanors by the police or the army in the name of the people. Thus the argument that the state has a prerogative to use violence internationally in a way that has no parallel in civil policing at home, and that this sets it morally apart, is false. In democratic societies, ethical responsibility rests squarely on the shoulders of the voters who elect governments to control armies and to oversee the administration of the law. This fundamental ethical line can and must be shaded at various points, but it cannot be obscured.

Against those who see the armed forces themselves as a source of violence and international tensions, it could even be argued (though not very seriously) that in real life the armies of most countries are less often employed in dispensing violence on a day to day basis than the average police force—a fact that, if anything, should make armies morally purer.

So once again, the disjunction between domestic and international morality—in this case in terms of the right to use violence—is unconvincing. The point can be extended almost indefinitely. Like the state, the individual citizen and householder has certain rights of self-defense—particularly starkly asserted in the case of gun law in the United States (often seen abroad, rightly or wrongly, as a reflection of the United States' no-nonsense stance in foreign affairs). The freedom of parents to resort to physical chastisement against their own children is another example, if one were needed. The point is so simple as to be almost redundant: If there is an "international jungle," we should contemplate the roots as well as the foliage.

The problem of the public presentation of policy and the need to appeal to raw feeling and prejudice to get the government's message across at all is the next in the list of factors that, it is argued, help to exempt statesmen, partially at least, from conventional moral rules. The difficulty is a real one. But it is surely as much a domestic as an international problem, a mundane part of the political process, conferring no moral dispensation on government, electors, or the media and imposing equal burdens on each: The media to inform, the elector to seek and sift information, and the government to be as open about the nation's confidences as is prudent for its security.

The relationship is thus between governments, the peo-

ple, and the press, television, or radio—and not simply between the government and the governed. The "Us" and
"Them" approach is morally far more comfortable, but it is
in nobody's interests to let the fourth estate off too easily.
The conventional view of those in power secreting or manipulating information for their own ends and of the media engaging in a fearless crusade for openness and honesty in the
interests of the public has an obvious glamor and the attractions of simplicity. In fact, the media have an important, if
often overlooked, ethical duty too—to provide accurate information and intelligent, rational commentary. Even more
frequently overlooked is the elector's own moral duty to require it.

All that said, it is certainly true that the presentation
of foreign policy can be more easily and more frequently
manipulated than the presentation of domestic policy. The
reasons are not hard to find; it is simply less easy for the
individual to check the facts. But more often it is less a case
of the media or politicians lying than of a certain mystifica-
tion of the foreign policy process. It is in too many people's
interests to elevate the element of power in international
relationships into some awe-inspiring alchemy whose se-
crets the man in the street can never hope to probe and
whose workings must remain beyond his control. Elemental
it can be; unfamiliar it is not.

The difficulty of imputing collective guilt to whole
states or peoples presents real difficulties for the philosopher or the lawyer. The acts of individual moral agents embedded in a particular institutional milieu, with its own
collective psychology and corporate defense mechanisms,
are an especially cloudy area. But the technicalities—
whether legal or philosophical—should not be allowed to
confuse the broader lines of the argument. In everyday language the notion of being "morally to blame" seems clear
enough, and the ambiguity of the use of the word "moral" is

a productive one: You may not have done the act, but you clearly connived in the action—probably by some form of Carlyle's "putrescent indolence."

Carlyle's judgment that the shoeblack and the sovereign are equally to blame for the French Revolution may seem hard on those who had no vote at the time. But in the case of the conduct of the foreign policy of a modern domestic state, the message is surely irrefutable: Namely that whether they like it or not, whole peoples are directly or indirectly responsible, together with their representatives, for misdemeanors against the legitimate interests of other peoples. If the people cannot be held to blame, who can?*

A standard objection to this thesis of popular responsibility is that electorates do not vote on foreign affairs. If that is the case, that is their privilege and their choice. Preoccupation with getting and spending, among other pastimes, naturally tends to override concerns about relations among states unless there is an international drama on hand to remind people. If indeed the public concentrates on parochial issues in elections, fails to vote at all, or does not participate in other ways in the foreign policy debate, it is expressing an indifference to events beyond its borders which entails certain moral consequences.

There may be sharp complaints and a good deal of breast-beating when things go wrong—when a famine occurs in Africa or when the consequences of long-standing neglect manifest themselves in Central America. But in both instances, corrective policies may demand a certain continuity of effort and some financial sacrifice. The public as a whole—as distinct from pressure groups—does not normally care enough to sustain the necessary interest and to force its concerns on the attention of governments. This is

---

*The notion of collective guilt can of course be finessed, but not always fruitfully. See, for example, "Morally Blaming Whole Populations" by Peter French (*Philosophy, Morality and International Affairs,* Oxford University Press, 1974).

neither surprising nor very interesting. It is perhaps a measure of the depth of current misconceptions, which find it convenient to attach guilt to governments rather than to face the wider and deeper problems of educating the electorate, that it needs to be stated at all.

Seen in this light, the final premise on which the whole construction of "differential morality" is built—that nations exist in an ethical stratosphere—subsides too. "The destiny of nations" comes to mean nothing more in the ethical argument than the will of a people expressed, in the case of a modern, Western nation, through the only available mechanism—democratic elections—by those who take the trouble to vote.

Once the simple principle is established, it can be instructive as well as entertaining to multiply demonstrations of the essential continuity in public and private behavior. Examples can be taken almost at random. Most people's lives are based on some form of more or less enlightened self-interest and ethical compromise. If subjected to the searching glare of public inquisition, their conduct could easily be made to seem at best pusillanimous, at worst downright immoral. Procrastination and indecision in states, like lethargy in individuals, is a mortal vice, and sins of omission are as popular among nations as individuals. Inertia mingles easily with self-interest and fear of change, and it is fear of change rather than wickedness that leads governments to maintain morally dubious relationships with hopelessly corrupt regimes: Central America is an obvious case in point. Statesmen share with other mortals the natural human fear of the unknown and are as inclined as any ordinary citizen to passivity, often under the illusion that passivity—the maintenance of the *status quo* —is itself a virtue. As Aristotle ironically notes, "Possession of goodness is thought to be compatible even with being asleep, or of leading a life of inactivity" *(Nicomachean Ethics,* p. 69).

It would be tedious to insist too much on the unity of human motivation, and the similarity of the ethical dilemmas faced by people in their public and private capacities. It is more diverting to look at matters the other way round; when we do, we see how the logic of discontinuity between individual and public standards can lead in strange directions.

The British writer, E. M. Forster, like many of those close to the Bloomsbury Group, was a pacifist. He also found the moral climate of his day restrictive—which is why Bloomsburyites were so influenced by Moore's *Principica Ethica*. A rather superficial reading of this work led to the attractive conclusion that, given the inherent difficulty of establishing rational moral norms, anything went. The only permanent virtues were seen as those of aesthetics, love, friendship, and pleasure. Forster's famous remark that he hoped he would have the courage to betray his country rather than his friends may be seen as a reflection of the moral despair of the World War I period; of the ever-fashionable view of the peculiar iniquity of governments; and of the clammy cliquishness and parochialism of Bloomsbury ethics, with its members' tendency to read their own subjectivity as intellectual intuition. But the implications of the observation are revealing. Presumably, despite his preference for friends rather than the abstract entities of nation states, Forster would have approved of international brotherhood. This raises the interesting question of whether he would betray friendly countries as easily as his own when they fall on hard times or misbehave, as friends and brothers do? Alternatively, does one stand by them right or wrong, as one does with friends? (Chile, Argentina, and the Philippines spring to mind.) Finally, what would Forster have done if faced with a choice between a friendly country and a friend? And is the only country it is right to betray one's own? It is not just a question of whether Forster would have the courage to betray his own country, or "friendly" countries: It is a question of whether he would be right or wrong.

These are not wholly frivolous matters. The dilemma that Forster resolved so confidently was less artificial than it seems. Bloomsbury morals lived on in the Apostles, a group of Cambridge undergraduates that included, among others, Anthony Blunt and Guy Burgess, both homosexuals who spied for Stalin and whose discovery was delayed for decades by a system of mutual self-protection, based on the "higher moral ground" of friendship.

It would of course be absurd to suggest that there is any facile equivalence between private and public morality. The differences, although entirely of degree, can be so marked as to appear qualitative. The first and most obvious is the lack of an effectual system of international sanctions against malefactors, an absence that can clearly embolden the adventurous and cause more law-abiding states to take prudent steps for self-protection, which may themselves appear threatening on occasion.

Many have dreamt of an international police force, but the recent operations of the United Nations peacekeeping forces have served mainly to underline the limits of what can be achieved. In the domestic life of countries, law-abiding conduct owes a good deal to fear of detection and punishment as well as to personal morality and the attractions of a civil society. States, on the other hand, are largely self-policing. Yet in certain ways the inhibitions to rash actions in the international arena are greater than at home.

Except for the most unstable Third World regimes, most countries, like individuals, will think carefully before provoking neighbors into disputes, confrontations, or war—especially if they are likely to lose. The peculiar difficulty in assessing the basis or likely consequences of one's actions in foreign affairs can also inhibit bad behavior as well as promote miscalculation. At this level, simple prudence can be a potent substitute for ethics. Moreover, unlike individuals, modern governments (not only in democratic countries) tend to go through ponderous deliberations before making decisions at all—the Soviet Union is the clearest example—and do not like taking chances. In representative democracies, careful thought has to be given to public reactions too. As a result, states can often (though by no means always) behave far less impetuously and more rationally than individuals, and the absence of a clear, effective means to restrain transgressors is not as big an inducement to misconduct as it might seem at first sight.

Uncertainty, in a world still uncomfortably close to the Hobbesian model, with its insistence on equal vulnerability, is perhaps the principal factor for restraint. The average state has as much, if not more, than the individual to gain in terms of security from observing "the law," written or not. Many of them do, most of the time. Most modern conflicts spring from civil wars and are frequently not fought among nations at all.

Perhaps the most conclusive proof of the thesis of this chapter lies in the behavior of modern representative democracies. For all their faults and the imperfections of their democratic systems, the stage of civil maturity they have reached is broadly reflected in the peaceable nature of their foreign policies toward each other. This still leaves room for criticism in East-West relations, of American action in Nicaragua or in the arms race, of Britain in the Falklands, or of France in Africa. All that is for discussion, and there is no conceivable case for complacency, as I seek to show later. But the plain fact remains that no two modern democratic states have gone to war between themselves, and there is little sign that they ever will.

5

THE
MORALISTIC
MEDIA

*The percept had swallowed up
the concept.*
—*ALDOUS HUXLEY,* The Doors of
Perception

▼

In *The Decline of the West,* Oswald Spengler notes that
gunpowder and printing had come into use at about the
same historical moment; that the appearance of the first fly-
sheets had coincided with that of the first field-guns; and
that the first mass firing of artillery, which took place at the
Battle of Valmy in 1788, a French victory over the Prus-
sians, was preceded by a tempest of propaganda pamphlets.
It is indeed a striking thought that the ability to broadcast
both death and the popular printed word matured and developed almost contemporaneously. Spengler calls them the
"two grand means of the Faustian distance tactics" *(Decline*

of the West, p. 394). He would have been highly gratified by the almost equally contemporaneous appearance of two even longer range and far more powerful weapons: Television and nuclear missiles.

The average elector, if he is interested at all, has simple instincts on foreign policy. But if these are to be translated into a healthy influence on governments, something more than instinct alone is required. If real morality subsumes practicality, it helps to know the facts. A simple solution is of course to leave the instincts to the people and for those in power to keep the facts to themselves. In effect and by no means always because of the villainy of governments, that is what can often happen. For both sides it can be a convenient division of responsibility—but it is a highly dangerous one.

This position is attractive because moral responsibility for policy decisions is implicitly shuffled off onto the politicians; it is dangerous because the two essential ingredients of an ethical foreign policy—right and reason, the moral urge and the need to live in the world as it is—are here divorced from each other. If democratic states are to function democratically in foreign as well as domestic affairs, the public must be informed and its mature opinions—not just its prejudices—relayed and reflected in the media and elsewhere for the edification of its elected representatives and governments.

To Kant and Mill, all this would have been a commonplace. A thinking electorate was at the heart of eighteenth-and-nineteenth century optimism—especially educational optimism—and it was still there in the early twentieth century too. In his autobiographical *The New Machiavelli,* H. G. Wells describes an idealistic friend who had determined to devote himself to a life of social improvement, especially in education. Wells quotes this friend as saying, "'Whatever matters or doesn't matter, it seems to me there is one thing we *must* have and increase, and that is the number of people who can think a little, and have'—he beamed again—'an adequate sense of causation'" *(The New Machiavelli,* p. 93). Eighteenth- and nineteenth-century rationalists and optimists found it hard to believe that anyone who knew the facts and had acquired an "adequate sense of causation" would vote for war.

Most people today gain their education on foreign affairs from the media. With our greater experience of their operations, many of us would now feel less idealistic and more cynical than Wells's young friend. We know, for example, that the line between the transmittal and transmutation of news and views is not easily drawn. We also now face the entirely new problem of pictorially transmitted information; the hopes of Kant, Mill, Wells, and others were based primarily on the more rational medium of print.

Most people are insulated from international reality not by governments or the media but by a real lack of interest, compounded by a perceived absence of relevance. For perfectly understandable reasons the average citizen is even less engaged by events beyond his borders than beyond his own town, hearth, and home. Even in the late twentieth century, his detachment is intensified by the equally natural assumption that the further such events are from him, the less able or obligated he is to react to them. And in the case of relatively self-sustaining economies like that of the United States it is not immediately clear to him just what he stands to gain by developing a closer acquaintance with life abroad.

He may nod when told that the globe is shrinking, but in his personal life he sees little clear evidence of that shrinkage: Through TV he can see things happening far away, yet somehow this does not bring them closer. The ethical implications of this gap in perception are interesting. Today, world events are thrust on everyone from the urban dweller to the remotest cottager through the resounding imagery of his TV screen. The impact of this relentless bombardment cannot fail to have some effects on his moral sensibilities. In the space of a single news bulletin, if he feels called upon to respond at all, he will be enjoined to stop other peoples' wars, punish international malefactors, rescue hostages, parry a new threat to national security, and bring succor to the world's suffering masses—to be a Samaritan, a Florence Nightingale, and a Saint George. Unless, that is, he retreats into a value-free aestheticism like the TV critic of the London *Times* who wrote the following: "The Vietnam War—the first on color television—still looks wonderful, with or without the doomy music made obligatory by *Apocalypse Now,* and this densely researched programme offered many visual treats."

Even as a citizen of a superpower, the average viewer is likely to become increasingly aware of the gap between the horrors he witnesses daily and his ability to do very much about them. It is this realization that must surely affect his behavior over time as a moral being. He can turn on himself in guilt, on his government in frustration, or on one of the foreign parties involved in easy condemnation. Alternatively—and more probably—he will turn away altogether, with a shrug and a sigh. Faced with this international deluge of moral disorder, for most people the most attractive options are anger or indifference, emotion or passivity.

Visually or orally, most individuals, in the West at least, are overwhelmed by the catastrophes of the world at every instant, in ways that do not necessarily reinforce their understanding of it. Not only are the subjects under discussion remote from the average citizen's personal experience; he has no ready means of verifying accuracy, even if inclined to do so, as is possible to some degree on other subjects such as the state of the domestic economy, where he can measure over time whether what he is told agrees with what he sees and hears. There is little incentive for and few direct means of discovering the facts about the news from abroad.

Inevitably too, there will be a predisposition among otherwise honest men and women to think the worst of foreigners. This banal, blatant, and normally innocuous chauvinism, sometimes indistinguishable from a healthy self-respecting patriotism, is easily inflamed at times of trouble or uncertainty into a more pernicious jingoism. Most people are only too ready to believe that someone is threatening them and to make reciprocal threats. Casually, inadvertently, or instinctively, the press, radio, and television play on these simple emotions.

But the media can play equally powerfully on other emotions too: Guilt, shame, and the urge for self-chastisement, as well as pride and self-assertiveness. Just as people can be encouraged to think the worst of others, so they can occasionally be enjoined to think the worst of themselves or their country too. It is characteristic of the Pietist with his tendency to ask "Who is to blame?" rather than "What is to be done?" to seek opportunities to reproach the United States itself for international disorders wherever possible, as though the ultimate source of the world's troubles lay in the corruption within one's own heart, rather than anyone else's. Such attitudes can be a form of moral conceit: Both chauvinistic pride and national self-flagellation are two sides of the moralistic coin. This is because both attitudes are often self-regarding, taking minimal account of external realities. They are just two among the many emotions that can be and are intensively exploited by the compulsive media. As early as 1831, Alexis de Tocqueville, in his *Democracy in America,* foresaw the risk that the growth of representative government might bring with it increasing vehemence and irrationality in the popular press. He notes that "The characteristics of the American journalist consist in an open and coarse appeal to the passions of his readers"

(Democracy in America, p. 94). Experience of today's visual media would seem unlikely to modify this view.

The average person in the Western world watches television for several hours a day. Since he or she is unlikely to spend the few remaining leisure hours ascertaining the accuracy of what they see and hear, it seems safe to conclude that many, if not most, people derive much of their most persuasive information on foreign affairs in picture form.

Nor should the influence of television on other media be forgotten: Both the press and radio are in competition with it, constantly striving for greater "picturesqueness" in their own presentation of information. The result is often to redouble the search for greater immediacy, greater vividness, and greater vehemence and to provide less sustained analysis even in the more reputable press.

The inherent limitations of television as a medium of enlightenment in politics in general are compounded in the case of foreign affairs. It is even less likely than in domestic matters to serve as a vehicle for reasoned discussion, and there can be no ethics without reason. Television, in a word, is by nature a moralistic medium.

Apologists frequently argue that, strictly speaking, its function is not to promote moderate, reasoned discussion on foreign affairs or on anything else; its job is to reflect reality in picture form, not to manufacture, analyze, or interpret it. If, for example, politicians choose in their television appearances to appeal to crude prejudices in their remarks on other countries and to reinforce these prejudices by theatrical artifice in presenting their views, so be it; the blame can hardly be laid at the door of the medium itself. As the Russians say, "Don't fume at the mirror if your mug is awry." Even if expensive, humiliating, or bloody consequences ensue in U.S. foreign policy from systematically emotive attitudes to a particular foreign country, the cameras will again not be to blame; indeed they will be there to monitor the consequences and to take credit for truthful, fearless reporting when "mistakes" in policy are eventually recognized and "corrected."

If we leave aside for a moment all questions of public duty, of selectivity in what is shown, of government control or interference, or of manipulation of access (which is to set aside a good deal), this claim to a sort of detached, benign amorality seems securely based. How can we blame the machine for what happens outside it? But like other assertions of technological neutralism, it needs closer examination.

Hans Morgenthau quotes in *Law, Morality and War in the Contemporary World* a casual remark by a U.S. airman who had been involved in high-level bombing missions over Vietnam to the effect that it felt as morally neutral as mending a television set. The man obviously chose his example at random, but the observation is evocative, partly for the reason Spengler saw in the simultaneous appearance of gunpowder and print: The importance of "Faustian distance tactics."

The airman's remark links the drama of bombing missions to humble domestic routine, and the link is technological. The ethical implications of modern technology are not confined to the use of weapons—to defoliants, intercontinental ballistic missiles, or the Strategic Defense Initiative. If it is accepted that men, rather than weapons, are the ultimate cause of war, it could be argued that the technology of communications has a greater potential for evil than that of chemical or nuclear weapons themselves, since it affects human motivation more directly than the mere existence of a particular weapons system. Television, as a "Faustian distance tactic," is at least as powerful as the weapons themselves. By acting as a source of heat rather than light on the subject of defense, for example, it could encourage the stockpiling of weapons in ever-increasing numbers or help to set a climate of political angst in which decisions to use them could come to be made.

The peculiar potency of television lies not in the wickedness of the journalists who operate the machine but in the very nature of the machine itself. Alone among other means of information, photography and film stake an implicit claim to absolute truth, and for all but the more sophisticated this claim is implicitly accepted. In fact, of course, the camera lies constantly, mostly inadvertently, and with total conviction. Lying is simply part of its essence: It cannot possibly live up to its pretensions of complete veracity. It is disjointed, impulsive, illogical; it can illuminate a point, distract, entertain, outrage, or intrigue the viewer. But the one thing it is most unlikely to do is to develop in him "an adequate sense of causation."

The primary function of the medium, as it is currently used, is to strike the mind by powerful selective imagery. Each image will seem totally persuasive, in a way in which mere words can never hope to match. It is this totality that is the source of its power, a power that can be disturbing. The impact on the eye and the brain can be as devastating and as unreasoning as that of a bomb on a city. (There are even analogies of idiom: The broadcaster speaks of "blanket coverage," just as the commander talks of "blanket bombing.") Both technologies strive towards the ultimate: Complete portrayal of "reality" in one case and complete obliteration of it in the other.

While implicitly asserting its absolute objectivity and comprehensive coverage, television is relentlessly anecdotal: It presents one corner of the reality of a given situation as the whole. Whatever its real importance, a single incident or moment in a battle is projected as symbolizing a wider truth, however unrepresentative or remote it may be from the central issue. That is why television is a prey to provincialism. But of course once broadcast, the event in question acquires a new prominence and *becomes* the "center of events"—the secret dream of every provincial coming up to town!

The same could be said of print or radio, but there is a

big difference. Only television has the power to *impose* itself on millions instantaneously as presenting the incontrovertible truth. A written reportage can mislead, sometimes willfully, but the printed word does not bring with it the illusion of absolute "reality," an illusion that is inseparable from photography. Inevitably, it will be countered that long-range photography has served an educative and therefore ethical function in foreign affairs by bringing distant realities closer and compelling us to take a view and shed our protective shield of unconcern. Surely television, it may be said, creates a useful illusion of proximity, making it harder than ever for modern statesmen or the modern public to echo the famous comment of the British Prime Minister, Neville Chamberlain, when Czechoslovakia was threatened by Adolf Hitler on the eve of World War II: That it was a faraway country of which we knew little. A more pertinent example in our own times of this line of argument might be the image of a starving child, a victim of war and famine in the horn of Africa. Will not such an image, in all its unspeakable pathos, bring home to a resident of Manchester or Chicago the "facts" of the situation and the need to do something to stop the war and to help the refugees, the sick and the starving?

The viewer's first reaction might well be one of immediate indignation that such a tragedy can happen at all. He may instinctively contrast the destitution of the child with his own affluence and feel stimulated to some concrete gesture of sympathy in the form of a generous personal contribution to the aid effort (though this may not be prolonged over time). He might be indignant that his own government is not doing more to help and would be in no mood to listen to the very serious arguments, deployed by humane and respected experts, against too much short-term aid to such countries.

More likely perhaps, the viewer's sensibilities may have been coarsened by a permanent succession of such pictures and by their habit of merging inextricably and irrationally into an endless fresco of other imagery, real or contrived. He may have been watching Bugs Bunny moments before. At the sight of the starving child, he may be tempted to switch back, his natural apathy reinforced by a comforting feeling of helplessness or by sheer genteel distaste at the sight. A suspicion may even cross his mind that he is being exploited politically—another incentive to evasion and inaction. Most insidiously of all, he may derive some momentary enjoyment from his own emotions of horror at the spectacle of starvation and from his indignation with his own government's inactivity, confuse this with genuine practical sympathy for the victims, and pass on his way.

Whatever the reaction, one thing seems certain: The image seems far more likely to provoke emotional concern than it is to enlighten the viewer about the real causes—political, diplomatic, economic, social, geographical, and historical—that have combined to produce the starving child. Except for a few rare cases, it is equally unlikely that it will promote any sustained, intelligent interest in these underlying problems. It is much more probable that it will produce a spasm of self-gratifying moralistic "concern."

It is questionable, then, how far the image itself can bring "the reality" of what is happening to the viewer. But nor will it leave that reality completely unimpaired; by selecting a single potent image or a series of images from a total situation that is often not composed of stimulating, visual material at all, but of a clutch of disparate factors, it will distort or destroy that reality in the imagination of millions of viewers. In other words, the true situation will neither be transferred to Manchester or to Chicago nor remain intact where it is, since it will be changed in the perception of countless millions. But the new "reality" will linger on, acquiring a life of its own, suspended in some intermediate limbo.

In his essay "The Thing," Martin Heidegger discusses the meaning of distance in the twentieth-century world. He foresees that television will definitively change the significance of the word. It will destroy the whole concept of "distance," imposing "a uniformity of non-distance in which everything will be carried away in confusion." Everything becomes equally near and far away, and thereby loses its true value and its very being: It exists only in a "nondistance" (p. 194).

All of us have experienced an inkling of what he means when we see in the flesh a famous cinema or television star or statesman: We cannot believe that we are really seeing the person or that he or she exists at all. The parallel with hallucinations and drugs comes to mind. Aldous Huxley once remarked about his experiment with the drug mescaline that, when looking at a chair while under its influence, he could no longer see it as a reality at all since "the percept had swallowed up the concept" (p. 194).

It is clearly important to beware of overstating the case. To revert to the horn of Africa, it is obviously true that some members of the public will react to the images of suffering by finding means to generate help for the victims, either through political action to hasten the search for diplomatic solutions, through more long-term aid to encourage self-help in the area, through a higher priority for Third World needs in the shaping of Western agricultural policies, or by more positive action through international agencies such as the United Nations. Even a short-lived upsurge of public consciousness and generosity is hard to scorn, despite those who argue that instant aid can do more harm than good: When asked why he insisted on pressing pennies into the hands of sleeping beggar boys on his doorstep, Dr. Johnson once said that it was to enable them to "beg on" (*Samuel Johnson*, p. 501).

One specific instance in which television is widely credited with a direct and, in many people's judgment, highly moral role in world affairs is in the ending of the Vietnam war. It is hard to deny the influence of television on public opinion in the United States or in other countries at the time or that the will of the American people and its government to persist in the conflict was eroded by the intrusion into American homes of horrifying scenes of battle and civilian casualties. To the average citizen the combination of fear for American lives and instinctive guilt at the suffering of the Vietnamese proved intolerable.

But even if we accept that television did help to shorten the war and that this had the result of saving lives on all sides, this does not necessarily tell us anything about the moral issue involved in the conflict itself, though it tells us a good deal about the power of television. It seems quite possible to suppose that the cameras could have stopped a thoroughly just war in precisely the same fashion: Americans would have been seen dying and using their superior technology to kill the enemy in just the same way. But the righteousness of the cause would have been hard to defend in the face of the visual "reality" about the war as transmitted on TV screens. (All this takes no account of the motives of the camera crew and others, though experience would suggest that they are unlikely to be predisposed in favor of the generals and the administration.)

Since war depends on national will, in the future it will probably be impossible for Western democracies to wage a war that is not central to their own survival for any length of time. The Falklands War may be seen as an exception to this rule; but it should be remembered both that it was in defense of British territory and British subjects and that the British government deliberately restricted television access to the battlefield—partly as a result of the lessons of Vietnam.

Those who might feel cheered at the prospect of reduced American involvement in the outside world (and this is a category that could include isolationists of both the Pietist and Brutalist tendencies) will no doubt take into account that Communist and other undemocratic countries suffer no such disabilities at the hands of the media. On the contrary, in the Soviet Union the moralizing powers of selective television imagery can be and have been used—in Afghanistan for example—to harden popular resolve, just as the effect can often be to soften it in the West.

Left to itself, in the West television will inevitably make its principal impact on two elements of the moral triad—the means and the consequences of a given action—to the exclusion of the third element—motives. The reason is simple: The means, which by definition must include violence, and the consequence, destruction, are visually exciting. Motives, praiseworthy or otherwise, are not, and they can only be presented verbally. Although television talks, its real language is pictures, and its more rational element—verbal description—has a secondary impact and status. It is astonishing how little people often retain about what is said on television: Mostly they are just looking. In that sense, television has not advanced far beyond silent films.

Even where motives are described, those who man the machine often find the temptation to create devastating discontinuities between "weak" verbally articulated aims and "strong" visually conveyed consequences of the most banal but persuasive kind irresistible. In the case of war it may or may not be true that "we went there to defend the peace," but what the viewer sees are selected images from those that happen to be available of the soldiers of a civilized, rational, and humane democracy killing peaceful civilians in an assault on an enemy-held village. For obvious reasons, there will be little balancing footage from the other side. Morally, therefore, the battle has been lost before it has begun.

But it would be wrong to take too narrow a view of the influence of television on military conflict. Although its articulation of motives may be "weak," it can have a potent effect through its imagery on the generation of political mood and motivation. Hence its effects are not confined to reporting wars: It could have a role in their making as well as in their prevention. It seems clear that television can help to stop wars—just or unjust. Can it help to start them too?

It would be interesting to examine the role of the media during the whole build-up of American political involvement in Indochina in the 1950s and 1960s. This was the time when the "China Lobby" was active, and the popular, demonic view of China at the time was a central determinant in U.S. decision-making. (It seems to us today an extraordinary thought that in the early 1960s a majority of United States public opinion was at one time in favor of using atomic weapons against China in defense of Quemoy and Matsu. How many people would be able to say where these islands are today?)

It would take a good deal of highly subjective research to establish the effect of television on the debate on China at the time, and the record of individual networks, producers, and commentators would no doubt show up differently in the pitiless light of retrospective judgment. But if we accept that much of American policy toward China was misconceived during much of the period preceding the Indochinese involvement and if we conclude that there was a dearth of cool, thoughtful, and objective discussion of the "Red China" issue during that time, certain conclusions about the media follow, even if one takes the view—which some will—that they were unduly subservient to the governments of the day.

The discussion is one of enormous complexity, the evidence likely to be highly diffuse, and the conclusions speculative. But on the basis of our own current, daily experience it is hard to allay the suspicion that the TV screen may have made its contribution to the over-heated political atmosphere on China during the formative years of United States policy towards Vietnam, less because the "beast" was under the wrong management—though some may argue that too—than because it is in the nature of the beast to exacerbate prejudice about a distant, complex, and alien reality rather than to promote understanding of it. It would be hollow praise indeed if television were to be applauded for "stopping the war" in Indochina if it could be shown to have contributed to the climate in which the war became possible. The fact that it may well have exerted useful pressure on the American government to extricate itself, with public support, from the consequences of a mistaken policy would hardly absolve the self-same medium from some rsponsibility, however indirect, for promoting the miscalculation in the first place, if such responsibility could be established.

Lest it be thought that this is some revisionist attempt to exculpate the chief culprits or evidence of a generally reactionary disposition against the modern media, it is worth noting the conclusion of the liberal historian and most experienced commentator on U.S.-Soviet relations, George F. Kennan, in a recent discussion of the prospects for an improved superpower relationship after the advent of Gorbachev:

> *The improvement of Soviet-American relations poses difficulties enough even when the attendant problems are viewed soberly and in life-sized dimensions. When everything has to be over-simplified, sensationalized, and blown up to dimensions two or three times beyond reality to meet the commercial demands of the press and television, the entire process of constructive statesmanship becomes subject to a heightened level of precariousness.*
>
> *Whether the process can successfully withstand these strains is a question [I am] able to answer optimistically only—one might say—on the brighter days.*

> *But in this political world, where artificially created images are considered more significant than realities, the unexpected is just as likely to assume favorable forms as unfavorable ones. It is always possible, then, that the irrational can provide hope where rationality perceives little reason for it ("The Gorbachev Prospect," p. 3).*

Kennan makes the essential point about the complete arbitrariness of much of the imagery we are subjected to perfectly.

It would be difficult and somewhat pointless to conclude from all this that television is an intrinsically infernal or immoral machine. But it is easier to see it as at best an amoral and at worst a moralistic means of communication: A natural vehicle for the Pietist or Brutalist view of the world. The mechanisms of pictorial representation, based as they are on naturalistic illusion, lend themselves all too easily to emotion and romantic extravagance. It is no secret that the chance availability of exciting illustration can sometimes shape the content as well as the form of a commentary. The selection of participants in discussion programs can also be made with an eye for theatricality, for heat rather than light, such programs being by definition visually unstimulating. The same can happen on radio, though the practice is more likely on the screen simply because the machine is not exploiting its full potential by displaying drab humans talking to one another; the pressure to heighten the drama by excited gestures, facial expressions, or raised voices is not one to be easily resisted by those in search of "good television."

The principal failing of television is that it can and does encourage simplistic, moralistic responses to complicated questions. It would be equally simplistic, however, to lay too many of our current ills at its door. Nothing is without its compensations, and even the small screen has the virtues of its own shortcomings. One of these is that, because of the compulsive power of the visual image that drives it, it may be less amenable to systematic control or manipulation than other media. Newspapers run carefully angled campaigns on this or that issue, undaunted by the evidence, and have even been known to report events that, in the words of a nineteenth-century American editor, "had not yet gone through the formality of taking place" (Boorstin, *The Americans,* p. 127).

It is less easy for television, in the West at least, to distort systematically: So enthralled is it to the availability of illustration that it finds it difficult to tame the urge to display its imagery, even if that imagery points in an unwelcome direction. It can and does overcook a discussion or a situation, but it is inherently less able (unless in totalitarian hands) to sustain systematic political bias over long periods (though it can intensify a national angst, as over China). It is at the mercy of its own preference for immediate sense impressions and anecdotal detail ("being on the spot") rather than for coherent, synthetic messages.

For this reason most Western governments, of whatever political complexion, are under the impression that the screen is permanently biased against them. In fact, left to itself, television is hostile to all political ideologies; it is by nature antinomian and anarchic: It breaks down reason into meaningless, visual "facts" that may frequently seem to conflict with or make a mockery of attempts by governments to project their policies as sober, consistent, and logical. In totalitarian countries and wherever there is enough control and a large and ruthless enough bureaucracy, the screen can of course by made to lie just as systematically and far more convincingly than print. But such is its power that it can also induce fear in the hands of those who control it. During the Cultural Revolution in China the television authorities themselves were so frightened of showing something that might inadvertently expose them to political crit-

icism that they resorted to the safest possible expedient:
The non-stop screening of texts and quotations from Mao's
Little Red Book.

This brief discussion has deliberately stressed the dangers of the visual media and sought to question the assumption that they are a medium of enlightenment as well as entertainment. There is no room for absolutist attitudes in this or other fields, and we have all seen and listened to TV programs made by intelligent, sophisticated, and honorable men and women that have sharpened our understanding of this or that aspect of international relations and that *have* succeeded, for us at least, in bringing distant realities closer.

It is also the case that some broadcasters themselves wish to use television in a more enlightened way than is often possible at present. But in the light of overall experience it is not easy to dispose of the main question mark over the medium as a whole. If the screen had only half the educative and curative powers some of its defenders ascribe to it and if it were only half as effective a vehicle for public enlightenment as we are sometimes told, given its hypnotic effect and the viewing hours of the public, we should be looking for evidence of a new era of humane understanding among mankind. As satellite broadcasting develops, we should also be looking for a new race of peaceable, global villagers. Yet somehow we are skeptical.

6

PIETISTS,
BRUTALISTS,
AND
INTELLECTUALS

*Morality is a synonym for
responsibility, and moralism is
conscious or unconscious escape
from accountability.*
—*ERNEST W. LEFEVER, "Moralism
and U. S. Foreign Policy"*

▼

Foreign policy is not made by the man or woman in the street. Nor is it made by their representatives, by ministries or governments, or by events. Like all other aspects of politics, it is an organic process. But within that organism, some elements wax and wane in strength and influence, and among those that appear to have increased over the years are those of the media and the intelligentsia, where Pietist and Brutalist attitudes are at least as rife as elsewhere.

It is sometimes said that the concept of organized dissent in politics by intellectuals emerged in its distinctive modern form at the time of the Dreyfus trial in France at the end of the nineteenth century. The exact moment when the phenomenon appeared can be disputed, and its roots can always be traced to earlier points in history: In eighteenth-century Britain Dr. Johnson and a number of his literary friends once got up a campaign to protect a wrongly accused Italian teacher. Whatever the roots of this tradition of political engagement by the intelligentsia, it appears to be acquiring a more systematic form, particularly perhaps in foreign affairs.

Until recently, the notion that academics, writers, poets, painters, actors, musicians, and dancers had a sort of weighted vote in the formation of a country's foreign or domestic policy went largely unchallenged, as many privileges do.* Despite our natural skepticism, we still find ourselves listening with perhaps more interest than they deserve to the impassioned views on the Middle East of a famous actress or to the recommendations of a professor of linguistics on the affairs of Israel or of South Africa. This deference to the political views of artists and thinkers is not confined to France and Germany, where intellectuals enjoy far higher public esteem than in most Western countries, but exists equally in societies not usually noted for their reverence for men or women of the mind. A number of explanations suggest themselves. One is perhaps that in Britain and America many find the opinions of intellectuals on politics more accessible than their works.

By virtue of their education, abilities, and critical awareness, such people tend by definition to have a healthy skepticism about official policy and, by virtue of their position, easier access to the facts. They are also likely to be

---

*The practice of this privilege is not without its risks. Even when he does not bite, the underdog can behave unpredictably. There is a story that, after it was all over, late in life, Dreyfus's contribution to a casual conversation on a newspaper report about an alleged spy was to remark sagely "no smoke without fire" (Guy Chapman, *The Dreyfus Trials,* p. 356).

more "concerned" in the best sense—that is, cerebrally as well as emotionally—about foreign policy. But none of this is any guarantee of a higher moral consciousness.

The writer, actor, or painter may also be more adept, because more articulate, at using foreign affairs as a stick to beat his least favorite politician or party, regardless of the rights and wrongs of the matter in dispute. He may also be dangerously unworldly; if he is a "liberal," he may, for example, be inclined to apply abstract, egalitarian norms to a world in which the exigencies of power are inescapable. He may also be constitutionally more likely to be attracted to Eldorados, forgetting the wise maxim of the British historian E. H. Carr that there will never be any approximation of Utopia if basic realities are ignored. He would certainly not think of himself as a "moralist," perhaps confusing the term with orthodoxy, stuffiness, and preachiness. Yet such he often is.

Despite such dangers, there is a persuasive enough case for giving greater attention—if not more weight—to the views on foreign affairs of distinguished men and women in the arts and sciences than to the man or woman in the street. However much they may abuse their privileged positions and however little they justify their implicit claim to be the conscience of a nation, we owe it to their distinction (or notoriety) at least to listen to what they have to say. But the "intelligentsia" has special responsibilities in return. The profession of part-time moral mentor to nations is a young one, and the record so far distinctly uneven. We need look no further than the history of intellectual attitudes to communism over the last few decades. By and large, they are a living reproach to generations of highly intelligent and well-meaning men and women. It is enough to glance back at the 1930s, 1940s, and 1950s to be overwhelmed with examples of credulity, irrationality, and stark irresponsibility that would be thought culpable in any other quarter. On East-West affairs, it is at least as easy to fault retrospectively the collective view of intellectuals over the last few decades as it is that of leading politicians of the same era.

Intellectuals also tend to change their spots even more frequently and drastically than politicians. Left-wing causes are now less modish. But it is striking that significant numbers of today's influential anti-Communists are former adherents of the ideology they now oppose with such spectacular venom. Converts from communism are always welcome, especially when they leave behind them that peculiar brand of intellectual intolerance that communism seems to foster. But this is not always the case, and the zeal of the convert is especially tiresome to those who never stood in need of conversion, who may include large numbers of less gifted but more balanced mortals.

This zeal becomes positively alarming when the converts in question exercise far greater influence on governments in their new faith than they did in the old, as was the case in the early years of both the Thatcher and Reagan administrations. And when the matter in hand is the elaboration of sane public policy toward the Soviet Union itself, with all that this means in terms of nuclear decision-making or defense budgeting, the humble man in the street may be forgiven for beginning to wonder whether government is not too serious a business to be influenced by intellectuals. When the Pietist turns Brutalist, it is time to take cover, especially when the Brutalist is closer to the throne.

But the left-wing totalitarian thinker turned right-wing policy adviser is an extreme—though by no means unknown—example. More typical and more revealing are the attitudes of individual non-Communist intellectuals to totalitarian countries. The reasons that drive many such people to take a more sympathetic view of the actions and motives of alien regimes than of those of their own governments and countrymen are many and various, but a distinctive feature in many instances is that these attitudes are often based less on an informed, critical involvement with the reality of the foreign country in question, than on an acute emotional and intellectual sensitivity to the painful shortcomings of their own.

Recent history teems with examples on both sides of the Atlantic. In Europe, the British writer Beatrice Webb and the Italian novelist Alberto Moravia have been among the most eloquent apologists for Russia and China. Born in 1858, the zenith of British power and prosperity, the daughter of a railway magnate, Beatrice Webb was a Fabian Socialist and an early sociologist. A woman of great intellectual energy, she was also deeply involved in social inquiry and political action, sometimes of the most vigorous, worthy, and practical kind. She was a tireless advocate, for example, of the benefits of good drainage to health. Like many people in her social position, she may have been guilty of taking a roseate view of the working class; but she also took a detailed, tough-minded and beneficial interest in the sluicing of the toilets in London's insanitary tenements. By any standards, she was a remarkable woman, who worked as hard as she read and wrote: "Read Taine's *Ancien Régime* with real enjoyment after ten days of artisans' dwellings Blue Books" *(My Apprenticeship,* p. 276) is a fairly typical entry in her diary.

In the 1930s she became closely involved with the Soviet Union and, after a long stay in the country with her husband, Sidney, produced a gigantic volume of over a thousand pages describing every aspect of Soviet society. What is interesting for us today is that the critical faculties and compassionate sympathy, which were rarely absent from her writings and work in Britain, deserted her almost completely in her writings on the Soviet Union. The depth of her illusions is best measured by the title of her book: *Soviet Communism: A New Civilization?* It is a bitter irony that the second edition, which appeared in 1937—the year of the Moscow trials—omitted the question mark.

This was not because Webb was unaware of what was happening. In a postscript to the second edition she includes a defense of the trials that is a small monument of intellectual dishonesty—a failing less easy to substantiate in her domestic writings. Suggesting nervously that it may appear "almost incredible" (p. 1152) to Western observers that some of Lenin's comrades turned out to be traitors, she goes on to argue that the trials may be the "inevitable aftermath of any long drawn-out revolutionary struggle that ends in a successful seizure of power" (p. 1157). She hunts for exonerating parallels from Western history and comes up with some strange samples: "The Scottish noblemen seemed to have conspired and killed, one side against the other, Protestant and Catholic, Whig and Covenanter, Hanoverian and Stuart, for almost a couple of centuries" (p. 1158). But most revealing of all, she quotes with approval the view of a "distinguished Irishman long resident in London" that Soviet justice may be of a higher-minded and purer sort than our own:

> . . . *the Russian prisoners simply behave rationally and sensibly, as Englishmen would, were they not virtually compelled by their highly artificial legal system to go through a routine which is useful to the accused only when there is some doubt as to the facts, or as to the guilt or innocence of the conduct in question. What possible good could it do them to behave otherwise? Why should they waste the time of the Court and disgrace themselves by prevaricating like pick-pockets merely to employ the barristers? (p. 1153).*

A Russian might quite understandably see our own judicial forms as a "farce, tolerated because our rules of evidence and forms of trial have never been systematically revised on rational lines" (p. 1153).

These last two words may be the clue to the origins of this dismal piece of intellectual perversion. Impatient with the incoherent muddle of British life and its slowness to progress toward a more orderly society ("Science, the Saviour of Mankind" is one chapter in her book), she could not allow the fate of a few individuals—intellectuals like herself or not—to stand in the way of her beliefs, and her determination to push, prod, and goad her own country toward a rational utopia.

In a strange way the Soviet Press at the time was more honest in its depiction of Soviet reality than the Webbs. The flavor of what was really going on in Russia is more accurately conveyed by the following excerpt from the Armenian newspaper *Kommunist* at the end of 1937. It describes the purge of "enemies of the people" conducted there by Anastas Ivanovich Mikoyan, one of the more "moderate" of Stalin's henchmen:

> *On the great Stalin's orders, Comrade Mikoyan rendered a great service to the Bolsheviks of Armenia in unmasking and rooting out the enemies of the Armenian people— the despicable bandits Amatuni, Buloyan, Akopov et al., who were forcing their way to the leadership with the aim of handing over the Armenian people to a cabal of landowners and capitalists.*
>
> *With passionate hatred for all enemies of socialism, Comrade Mikoyan ably assisted the Armenian people, and on the great Stalin's orders he personally helped the workers and peasants of Armenia to unmask and destroy their base enemies, the Trotskyist-Bukharinist, Dashnak-Nationalist spies, who were wrecking workers' and peasants' Armenia . . .*
>
> *It was Mikoyan who, on the orders of the great Stalin, exposed and threw out the workers' sworn enemies, the Trotskyists and Dashnaks, Amatuni, Akopov, Guloyan, Zhugdusi and other riff-raff.*

In size and significance *Soviet Communism: A New Civilization* is a masterpiece of misunderstanding of the realities of life in a foreign country, even though it is replete with every sort of "fact." Thus, two highly intelligent and naturally skeptical thinkers, who would never have dreamt of accepting without reserve the policy explanations of their own elected government, reproduce the official description of life and labor in Soviet Russia with scarcely a murmur of inquiry or dissent. This was not because they were puppets of the Soviet regime. They were simply not concerned with Russia as it was for the Russians, but only with the Soviet Union as a model for "a new civilization." Their work is not just a gigantic slab of moralizing, earnestly directed at a British audience and intended to uplift its ideals; it is also an immoral book because what is missing is the humanity and concern for the individual the Webbs displayed at home.

The Webbs' tome, a milestone—now a tombstone—of its genre, is neither the first nor the last example of discontinuities of moral judgment that otherwise sane intellectuals are in the habit of bringing to foreign affairs. A more recent instance is the romantic indulgence shown by liberal opinion in the West to the brutal obscurantism of the Cultural Revolution in China. The first victims of the upheaval were critics and writers, and later a paroxysm of anti-intellectualism seized the entire country. While professors were being beaten up by their students, and opera singers, musicians, and painters were reviled and sometimes driven to suicide or murdered, sensitive and thoughtful people in the West were writing apologetically or even enthusiastically about Mao's Red Guards and his policy of "smashing the old." In his *Reflections on the French Revolution* Edmund Burke prophesied that "the men who today snatched the worst criminals from justice will murder the most innocent persons tomorrow." He was writing about the tendency of some intellectuals to base their morality on vaporous feelings of "benevolence," and in today's circumstances undue benevolence towards some distant regimes involves condoning murder, made all the easier when the "innocent persons" in question happen to be foreigners.

Alberto Moravia is one of the few Western writers to have visited China during Chairman Mao's last revolutionary spasm. The book that he wrote as a result of his visit was far lighter in size, scope, and tone than that produced by the industrious British sociologists after their stay in Russia. But the import is remarkably similar.

Moravia visited China in 1967, just over thirty years after Beatrice Webb's book on the Soviet Union. But there are broad historical parallels in the situation of the two countries. Both the Russian and Chinese Revolutions were going through heightened phases of repression at the time. Moravia and the Webbs were therefore dealing with Communist regimes at their most pitiless, and their reactions are therefore doubly worth scrutinizing.

Moravia gives an account of his brief stay in *The Red Book and the Great Wall—An Impression of Mao's China*. His writing is certainly more fetching than that of the Webbs, and he offers an intelligent and perceptive account of the Cultural Revolution. Even the ubiquitous banalities of the period—the posters, the banners, the slogans—are given greater meaning by Moravia's observations. He has an extraordinary non-meeting with a Chinese writer who agrees that there are good things in Tolstoy (though he "has the limitations of his century"), dismisses Shakespeare as "a bourgeois writer," and has never heard of James Joyce. Moravia muses on the Great Wall, on the Revolution's hatred of the past, and on China's apparent lack of interest in the West. Many of his reactions—particularly his view that Mao was attempting to replace a Confucian by a revolutionary conservatism—expand our understanding of events.

But of greater interest are the author's moral impressions about the Revolution, conveyed somewhat coyly through a sort of Socratic dialogue at the beginning of the book. He is struck and impressed above all by its exaltation of poverty:

> *. . . for me, China today is a Utopia that has been achieved, perhaps involuntarily, perhaps by chance, it makes no difference. . . . Later, perhaps, China will become a country like all others, including the Communist countries of the Soviet persuasion, in which there are the poor because there are the rich and vice-versa. But for now, today, China is a poor country without rich people, that is, a country in which poverty is synonymous with normality (p. 10).*

Moravia notes that Christianity managed to exalt poverty as an ideal state for only a few centuries. Modern Western civilization, he says, is now obsessed with consumption, which he equates with excrement: "Consumer civilization is excremental. The amount of excrement discharged by the consumer is actually the best proof that the consumer has consumed" (p. 17).

Western culture is "excremental" too, consumed in the same way as industrial products: "ingested, digested and discharged in an immense quantity of excremental commonplaces" (p. 18). One simple way to limit the appetite of the consumers is to limit their number; that is, by chastity. Moravia suggests that poverty and chastity—central themes of the Cultural Revolution—are the only ways to prevent mankind degenerating further through the producer-consumer cycles.

The important thing about Moravia's highly generalized conclusions is that they tell us far more about Europe's problems than China's solutions. They reflect a certain moral repugnance at the rampant consumerism and sexual license of the 1960s in the West, though by no stretch of the imagination could it be claimed that these were among China's most pressing national problems in the pre-Cultural Revolution era; rather the contrary if, that is, you happen to be a Chinese. Read retrospectively, Moravia's book is therefore more informative about Italian than about Chinese states of mind. The underlying preoccupation of the author with his own country surfaces in the prose; Canton's arcades remind him of Bologna: "A Chinese Bologna drowned in the humidity, sultriness, and delirious promiscuity of the tropics" (p. 31). Even the *da tse pao* (the big character posters) pasted over each other, layer upon layer, suggest to him Italian *millefoglie* pastries.

Most probably the author saw himself as writing a sympathetic account of China and the Chinese; yet he shows not the slightest compassion for the sufferings of his fellow intellectuals under the vicious campaign of the "Gang of Four" led by Mao's wife, the lamentable Jiang Ching. His book should be reread alongside the harrowing accounts that we now have of the personal tragedies of the victims of the Revolution—not least of young writers and artists.

But this does not mean that Moravia is unfeeling. China, for Moravia, is not really a human entity at all, but merely an object of political and cultural fantasy, an intellectual plaything, whose citizens are not credited with any inner life, frustrations, or passions; they are deemed, instead, to enjoy some subliminal contentment with their chaste, non-consumer's lot. In this sense, despite the quality of the writing, the book is a work of high vulgarization, since it accepts—as many superficial journalistic accounts have done—that the Chinese really are the automata that they can appear to be when they are coerced into external uniformity.

Like Webb, Moravia—whose writing on his own society betrays understanding and feeling enough for the distress of his fellow mortals—seems blind to the misery, material or intellectual, imposed by a totalitarian society on its victims. That misery has now been poignantly recorded in the writings of the generation who themselves underwent the Cultural Revolution. One, a poet called Gu Cheng, wrote a poem in March 1980 called "A Generation," which encapsulates the whole experience in two lines:

> *The night has given me dark eyes.*
> *But I use them to look for light.*

The Webbs did not live long enough to read *Dr. Zhivago,* but it is sincerely to be hoped that Moravia reads Gu Cheng's poetry.

The United States' own contribution to the history of political self-deception by some of the most gifted Western intellects and authors, often springing from urgent concerns with the state of things at home, has been brilliantly charted in Daniel Aaron's book *Writers on the Left.*

At the same inauspicious moment as the Webbs were confidently removing the qualifying question mark from the title of their work, Upton Sinclair was sending his personal revolutionary greetings to the Soviet government, whom he congratulated in particular with solving the problem of the national minorities and, even more ironically from today's vantage point, of drunkenness. Even allowing for hindsight and the reaction of many Western intellectuals at the time to the rise of Hitler, his enthusiasm for Stalin's achievements seems distinctly over-exuberant and ill-omened today.

There is perhaps more excuse for Theodore Dreiser, whose *Dreiser Looks at Russia* had appeared a decade before in 1928. The appalling excesses of the Soviet system were less evident in 1927, when he spent eleven weeks travelling in Russia, than ten years later. There is also far more humanity and humor in Dreiser's account than in those of some other sympathizers with the Revolution. He made plain his dislike of the operations of the GPU (the KGB of the time)—"There is a kind of terror that lies in secret methods which chills the heart of man" (p. 128)—and of the techniques of thought control—"the endless outpour and downpour of progaganda" (p. 89). But despite all his good sense and zestful criticism, he finds the regime fundamentally attractive: "Not a city, not a village or hamlet in all Russia today . . . is not feeling the thrill of the new intellectual and social life emanating from the new leaders and theorists in Moscow" (p. 88).

In his own rangy way, Dreiser uses his experiences to moralize at the American people. Sex is better in Russia because more natural: none of the "infernal newspaper racket" over divorce, breach of promise, and alimony, which helps to "while away the hours of the mentally unemployed" in his own country (p. 20). He sees want and squalor but none of that "haunting sense of poverty or complete defeat that so distresses one in western Europe or America." Even Moscow's beggars are "more picturesque" (p. 26). Despite the dirt and the laziness, he sees an intellectual and spiritual superiority in Russia. In their mental or emotional lives, most Americans, in his view, get out of the thirty-two floor elevator at the tenth floor; most Russians ascend further, "all being more interested in what is above than what is below" (p. 51). As for indoctrination in education—"But what of it? Are not Americans being taught the perfection of capitalism, the Italians that of Fascism, and the Spaniards that of Catholicism, and so on!" (p. 101).

Like the Webbs, he comments on the Soviet legal system, under which a man brought to justice is assumed to be guilty unless proved innocent. He is honest enough to wonder how many innocent men are convicted or freed. But he also shares some of the Webbs' relief at a system that does away with the tiresome complexities of the Western way of doing things: "How simply Russia gets rid of such harpy band of lawyers, sharpers, technical experts, etcetera etcetera as invariably infests and befogs every trial here!" (p. 118).

Dreiser's book, unlike so many others in the genre, at least beats with a warm human pulse. He approves of the experiment, but does not overlook the sufferings of those undergoing it. The moralizing theme in his book, to which he returns time and again, whether on education or in a comparison between the Russian and American temperaments, is concerned less perhaps with politics than with the superiority of the Russian "soul." Unlike the Americans, with their stunted materialism, the rulers of the Russians are aspiring to a higher world of "intellectual leisure" once they have succeeded—which he has no doubt they will through the Revolution—in acquiring the necessities of life for their people. The judgment—forgivable in its American generosity (surely an agreeable aspect of the American "soul" too?)—was wildly mistaken on both counts. As Soviet intellectuals have had cause to know, the mode of government that Dreiser, on balance, approved has combined economic penury with spiritual debasement.

Truly ethical attitudes to foreign policy cannot be divorced from the interests of the peoples of other countries. It must therefore be immoral—or at best moralistic—to use them and their peoples as mere symbols, models, or sources of ideological stimulation, still more as pawns in a national political game. Where the interest in the country in question is clearly self-serving, totemic, or quite simply opportunistic, we are dealing with moralism in one of its most distasteful and pernicious forms.

The most striking recent instance of the effects on foreign policy attitudes of internal climates of intellectual opinion is in France. Within little more than a decade there has been an almost complete reversal of French intellectual attitudes to the Soviet Union from sympathy to almost universal opprobrium. Paris suddenly discovered the *gulag* many years after its appearance in Russia. Nothing new had happened within Russia to bring about this change of perception—though the Soviet invasion of Afghanistan and its pressures on Poland gave it greater impetus. It was almost entirely the product of French domestic politics, the decline of the French Communist party, and the rise of the socialists—plus perhaps the boredom factor. The intellectual flirtation with Russia had been going on a long time and was growing stale with age. It was time for a change.

Jean-Paul Sartre on Russia; Louis Ferdinand Céline and Ezra Pound on Nazi Germany; Noam Chomsky on the Holocaust—the list of otherwise brilliant people whose resentment of the inadequacies or injustices of their own countries led them into extraordinary mental contortions or severe misjudgments in their assessment of other societies is endless. Obviously, full account must be taken of individual circumstances, of historical context, and perhaps of the heightened awareness of superior intelligences that leads, paradoxically, to cerebral passion gaining the upper hand over reason and empirical fact. But it is a dismal catalogue, nonetheless.

We understand, of course, what these writers were seeking—an external answer to the problems of their own societies. This search for the "true faith"—scientific communism in Russia, the puritanism of China, or the heroic might of national socialism—is part of a long tradition epitomized in the legend of Prester John, the fictional saintly ruler of "the three Indies," where honey, milk, peace, and justice were equally abundant. It is a legend that held a tenacious grip on the early medieval imagination, to the point where the paradise actually featured on some maps at the time. At one stage in the thirteenth century it seemed that Prester John himself had at last been identified. Unfortunately—and significantly for our purposes—it transpired that there had been some confusion with Genghis Khan.

Such confusions are less forgivable in the twentieth century. Stalin, Mao, Hitler, and Castro are stern enough realities, and their deeds were there to be assessed during their own lifetimes. Writers and artists deserve no more moral indulgence—if anything, less—than humbler mortals, including politicians or diplomats, for shutting their eyes to inconvenient truths.

Not all cases of political myopia spring from idealistic high-mindedness or intellectual perversion. Simpler human frailties, such as plain gullibility, play their part too. Malcolm Muggeridge, a British journalist, describes in his book *The Thirties* an entertaining instance that occurred when George Bernard Shaw was visiting Russia at a time of rumored food shortages (p. 79). Shaw had prudently taken with him a supply of canned meat. On arrival in Moscow, he described with great satisfaction to his audience how he had thrown his provisions from a train window, having decided that all the talk of shortages was mere propaganda, adding that he had never been so overstuffed in his life since coming to Moscow. The feelings of his listeners at this announcement—many of whom may themselves have been on short rations—can easily be pictured. The image of the cans lying alongside the track is an abiding symbol of the occasional fatuity of great minds.

7

THE
ETHICS
OF
INTERNATIONAL
ACTIVISM

*Bustling folly is the character
of our species.*
—*IMMANUEL KANT,* **Idea For A
Universal History**

*Little fraternities and co-partner-
ships—weak ties indeed, and what
may afford enough for ridicule.*
—*BISHOP JOSEPH BUTLER,*
Fifteen Sermons

▼

How much time and effort is it right for a country to
spend on foreign affairs? How many countries need a foreign policy at all? And if global cooperation is a worthy chi-
mera, do regional partnerships among clusters of countries
present equivalent dangers of self-gratifying "bustling" activity on a smaller scale?

A critique of over-activism in international relations is
not difficult to formulate. In recent years there has been an
enormous inflation of "business." The geometrical increase
in the number of mutual visits, conferences, summits, and
statements seems to the casual observer to have no correla-

tion with the number of problems solved or with those susceptible of solution. There are, of course, simple practical explanations: It is now all too easy for statesmen and diplomats to move themselves and their cables around the world, regardless of how much either have to say. The club of sovereign nations has also expanded sharply as former dependencies have become self-ruling. Semi-automatic membership of myriad international organizations brings instant involvement in foreign policy even to small and remote territories. These are immediately courted on independence, if only for their vote, by this or that established group or country, like young girls at a coming-of-age party.

Newly independent states naturally like to assert their independence; older ones have become addicted to diplomacy as a bureaucratic emanation of the state. New and old therefore tend to exaggerate their interests or their responsibilities, as their statesmen seize the opportunities the media offer to dance like flies in the beam of public attention.

How far does this business in foreign policy promote or damage the interests of the international community or indeed of the activist himself? How much of this activism comes under our broad definition of moralism? In the case of the developed countries of the West, there is a strange contradiction between the current tendency of governments to seek to diminish their role wherever possible in the regulation of the life of the individual and the tendency of their leaders to involve their countries in ever more international activity.*

In some non-Western countries there is all too much

---

*In the early post-World War II years, T.S. Eliot saw the dangers when he wondered how healthy it was for governments to be involved in sending representatives of the arts and sciences abroad and inviting foreign representatives to their countries. He expressed the hope that intellectuals would increasingly travel as private citizens and make each other's acquaintance without the approval and support of official organizations (*Notes Towards the Definition of Culture,* p. 94).

evidence that a period of Buddhist self-contemplation at home might be more fruitful than over-involvement in the international arena. Too much self-assertion in a nation, as in an individual, whether it consists in simple busybodying or, more dangerously, fiddling with frontiers, seems unlikely to promote the general welfare. The idea that any form of international (or for that matter community) activity is good for its own sake is doubtful and is at least as open to abuse as any other form of cooperative endeavor: The sad degeneration of the most inspirational aspect of the United Nations, UNESCO, is the most striking *memento mori* of the international ideal.

Consciously or otherwise, foreign affairs are used as an escape valve in peacetime as well as in war. Just as rulers might once have sought to distract a restless populace by adventures abroad, so many modern leaders jostle for prominence in keeping the peace. Self-aggrandizement can thus mix with escapism, to no great advantage to the world and with the risk of encouraging illusions about oneself or others. The most reliable unit of peace is a prosperous, educated, stable democratic nation. It is not difficult to think of countries whose prosperity, cultural level, and democratic credentials might be enhanced by a more rational distribution of the energies of their leaders. The benefits to the international community of a more determined approach to domestic economic problems could include more trade and less diplomatic wave-making.

Diplomatic discussions with no specific purpose or result can be a harmful form of self-indulgence, leading among other things to the striking of moralistic attitudes on highly generalized issues or to nations being led astray by their leaders, who are determined to be seen to be involved in the solution of problems for which they have no direct responsibility. Never before has there been such a plethora of eager international "mediators" on permanent standby.

It is salutary to recall that the most successful diplomatic conference of modern times—the Lancaster House negotiations over the independence of Rhodesia—achieved a solution partly by rigorously restricting attendance to those with a direct practical and moral responsibility for the problem—Britain and the internal Rhodesian parties, black and white. The Commonwealth, the "Front Line States" (including Zambia, Tanzania, Mozambique, and Nigeria), and even the United States were physically barred from Lancaster House from start to finish, and their role in the wings was restricted to an essential minimum. In this way those with a functional and ethical duty to reach agreement were placed squarely before their obligations and prevented from backing away towards some wider, diffuse, and unattainable "consensus."

Countries, like people, get in with bad company; the group dynamics of diplomacy are not always the straightest path to virtue. As for the supposed value of "meeting people," there are countries that could have developed more stable relationships if only their leaders had never encountered one another. Sometimes the unavoidable conclusion seems to be that the best contribution many countries, large or small, can make to world peace is to stay out of the global village unless they have good reason to be there. The fact that it is far easier to make a speech on foreign than on domestic policy should put us on our guard. In a word, diplomacy could be yet another area of modern life where less means better.

Purely on the level of newspaper reports, the instinctive impression that too much is happening is difficult to shake off. The ethical aspect of this impression is not confined to the suspicion that, because statesmen clearly enjoy international activity so much, it must be sinful and damaging to someone's interests. Immoderation of any kind, even with the best of intentions, automatically becomes a bad thing. Given the severe natural limits of what can be achieved at any one moment in foreign policy, the states-man's duty to avoid "over-government" abroad is at least as binding as it is at home. Less frequent appearances on the international stage could leave the leaders of many countries, large and small, with greater time for reflection—and for rehearsal.

Regrettably there are counter-arguments, mostly in the form of tiresome truisms. Greater economic interdependence brings increased political intercourse: The elaboration of the law of the sea is an obvious example. An active foreign policy is seen by new nations as an external complement to their personalities as states. Isolation or (in the case of larger and more experienced states) introversion carry their own dangers. Greater economic activity by statesmen at home could in some circumstances make matters there even worse. Most excess foreign policy is harmless and relatively cheap.

It is sometimes better for statesmen to meet, even if they have nothing to say, than to mix ignorance with inherited resentments and suspicions. By these contacts they will add a fragment or two to their own and to their country's store of wisdom and even perhaps be usefully impressed by the inherent complexity of international relationships and hence the need for prudence and restraint. Both regional cooperation and multilateral diplomacy, which are developing fast, are inevitably complex, manpower-intensive, and by their nature "busy." The interminable Helsinki process between East and West, a less glittering successor of the Congress of Vienna, suggests that we may have entered the era of the bureaucratization of the peace.

So a degree of international busybodying is inescapable. But a vital distinction should be drawn between global and regional patterns of activism. The world has never been short of idealistic schemes to secure international partnership, and lasting peace. In the second half of the twentieth century many hopes have rested on the United Nations, and some still believe that the organization should be given both the power to legislate and its own enforcement agencies. At the very least, such notions present awesome difficulties of implementation, and the record of the United Nations to date gives few grounds for extravagant expectations. This is not in itself a reason for cynicism towards the only established means we at present possess of harmonizing the contending interests of established states, for abandoning the search for global patterns of cooperation, or for the strengthening of the rule of international law. But there are powerful arguments for not putting too much of one's faith in early progress and for devoting energy meanwhile to what can be achieved nearer at home and in a shorter time scale. Such rank empiricism will not be popular among theoreticians of the absolute, but we must start where we can.

Internationally, perhaps the highest practical form of political morality is free cooperation among sovereign states, of a kind that is not directed against the legitimate interests of other countries. One of the most positive developments in the international arena in the last few decades has been the slow but steady emergence of patterns of regional cooperation in various parts of the world. The motives of the countries concerned are varied, and the element of idealism has been less evident than the self-interested search for security and economic advantage. Again, Western Europe springs to mind: With the rapidly lengthening shadow cast before it by expansionist Soviet power, not to speak of the prospect of economic penury unless it created its own internal market, the political incentive to united action was clear enough. The Association of South East Asian Nations (ASEAN), an area with a similar history of recent conflict, and whose countries are dwarfed by the bulk of China, was inspired by broadly parallel motivations. In the Nordic countries and in more embryonic form in Africa, Central America, and the Persian Gulf similar groupings have sprung up or are developing. (There are Communist counterparts too, though the regional "fraternities" of Eastern Europe and Southeast Asia are dominated and controlled by a single country—the Soviet Union or Vietnam. They can, therefore, be more accurately described as new types of imperialism rather than new forms of voluntary association.)

Young as it is—it is not yet forty—the European Economic Community is the most mature and sophisticated of these regional associations. The overwhelmingly economic character of the Treaty of Rome has sometimes been seen as constricting its development. But one of the earliest European attempts to formulate international cooperation—the maritime codes of the early Middle Ages—sprang from economic interests. One of the first writers on international law, Hugo Grotius, began work on international law when he was asked by the Dutch East India Company to compile a treatise to justify the seizure of a Portuguese merchantman.

In the everyday life of the European Economic Community, the "practice of virtue" is not always an edifying spectacle: The self-seeking of its component states too often shows through the more high-minded appeals to common endeavor, not least in the attempts to coordinate a workable agricultural policy. (Heidegger's warning about collective action only aggravating nationalism is again pertinent here.) But if ethics is essentially habit, moral virtue is largely the result of steady, cumulative effort. What is most significant about the Community, in our present context, is the routine habit of cooperation in other fields that has developed alongside economic cooperation, even though it was never formally enshrined in the Treaty of Rome.

One of the least publicized but most notable achievements of the Community is the establishment of the practice of permanent political cooperation at every level of government—official, ministerial, and among heads of state. This has not overcome rivalry between individual European states, but it has promoted a gradual realization of a wider common interest. If a crisis blows up somewhere in the world today, the instinctive reaction of the new generation of junior diplomats at the Quai d'Orsay in Paris, the British Foreign Office, or the German Foreign Ministry in Bonn is to telephone each other to discuss how Europe can manage the problem, rather than think of ways they can exploit it and use it against each other. Nor should the effects of frequent personal meetings among ministers and heads of state be underestimated, though it would be naive to suppose that such contacts are invariably bathed in sweetness and light, or that they always serve a concrete purpose. Again, despite the element of self-indulgence, it is the habit of meeting that matters. It is partly because of this evolving ethos of communal consultation and action that it is now almost impossible, forty years after World War II, to envisage a new conflict among Western European nations.

The spirit of this cooperation is frankly gradualist and prudential, and the experiment proceeds crablike by a series of compromises, both economic, political, and occasionally—as in the Community's less obviously successful dealings with terrorism—moral.

It is impossible to deny that it represents something of a rich man's club, though it is not clear what poorer countries would gain from a poorer Europe; they would certainly lose a great deal of trade and in some cases a political and military counterbalance to the Communist block. Moreover, the Community's awareness of its wider international duties is reflected in extensive tariff arrangements (the Lomé convention) with the Third World and in Community aid programs that complement those of national governments.

The utopian critic—if he has any sense of gratitude—should also note other contributions to international virtue made by the Community in its few years of existence. Besides contributing to the maintenance of peace in Europe for nearly half a century and promoting the economic and social welfare of its citizens as well as greater political stability than they would otherwise have enjoyed, it has helped to blunt the sharper edges of European nationalisms, partly by establishing the principle of supra-national legislation. This has so far been cautiously confined to economic and social areas, and even here the last word is frequently and sensibly left with national parliaments.

It is in the interactions between these individual parliaments—the ultimate guardians of sovereignty in each country—and the European Economic Community as a whole, that the real nerve-centers of Community action lie. Each national assembly has developed tight procedures for scrutinizing European legislation in order to ensure that controversial measures do not get so far ahead of public opinion as to expose governments to a nationalistic backlash, which might threaten membership of the Community itself. But behind all this is the overriding political and economic self-interest of member states in continued association. In the present and in any foreseeable international context it is not easy to see how any major member of the Community could make its way outside it. Even in the United Kingdom, where a certain ambivalence about membership still lingers, this fundamental truth is increasingly widely recognized.

The Community has also promoted far greater freedom of movement (Kant's "universal hospitality"), employment, and residence than existed before. Historically, this may not be so great an innovation when measured against the intensive cultural and other exchanges of earlier centuries that were not organized by governments, but that it has been of great practical and economic benefit is not open to doubt.

The Brutalist critic would find it hard to disapprove of

the principle of European association. But he would be bound by the logic of his own essential pessimism to see it as an evanescent phenomenon, to be rent apart in due course by the divergent interests of its components or, alternatively, to be dominated by one of its more powerful members. There are strains and contradictions enough inside and outside the EEC—the over-reliance on the United States for the Community's defense being the most obvious, not to speak of the potent ambiguities of a still divided Germany. Despite these latent tensions and the pressure generated by economic recession, the countervailing forces of communal advantage seem to have secured a remarkable degree of coherence.

The "realist" might then point with quiet relish to the prospect of inevitable clashes in a world dominated by such regional groups. It is true that, however remote at present, the notion of conflicts among blocs is no less disturbing than that of war among states. It is equally true that the economic skirmishings between Brussels and Washington have been frequent and sometimes bitter. By their very structure, however, such associations of countries are less likely to be driven by the less refined, more primitive instincts of the nation-state. The very divergence of interest among their members mutes any conflict of this kind and favors compromise. Such flexibility has already been apparent in the relationships between the European Economic Community and ASEAN.

International egalitarian moralists, for their part, should take particular note of the way the system protects the interests of "minority" countries—Belgium, Holland, Luxembourg, or Greece. The unavoidable conflicts of interest between member states of widely differing sizes—they range from Germany's sixty-five million inhabitants to five hundred thousand in Luxembourg—are real enough. But they are mitigated by a presidency that rotates among big

and small members alike and by procedures for joint decisions that are carefully contrived to allow countries the
right of veto in exceptional circumstances.

It would be completely unrealistic and would lead to
the early dissolution of the Community if every member,
irrespective of size and influence, had equal voting rights.
(This is not even true in the United Nations, if account is
taken of how its principal organ, the Security Council, is
constituted.) The result in Europe is a complex system of
weighted voting that reflects the importance of the larger
countries while not leaving the smaller ones at a disadvan-
tage. In this sense, it is a perfect illustration of John Rawls's
second principle in practice: Inequalities are accepted as
beneficial to all and regulated in a manner that encourages
cooperation among large and small powers.

One aspect of the Community would appall realists and
Utopians alike: The proliferation of its bureaucracy. It is
unfortunately a mathematical fact that the concentration of
economic, social, or foreign policies among so many sovereign countries will bring with it almost infinite permutations of committees, votes, resolutions, and legalisms that
sometimes seem to be of a disabling complexity. Those who
favor the minimal state and see over-government as immoral will find difficulty in reconciling this aversion with
any desire for realistic international cooperation. Democracy itself is of necessity an untidy and time-consuming
business, and there can be no neat compacting of cooperative procedures among democratic states. This is an area
where economies of scale do not seem to operate. No one
who has had any dealings with the EEC will be unaware of
the need to avoid extinguishing the sparks of idealism beneath the heavy dread of officialdom.

The emergence of regionalism in its twentieth-century
form is bringing a new practice into international affairs
that finds meaning and a form of morality in the contextual

patchwork of a shared culture and history and in the coordination of economic and political objectives within a limited area. It will work best among groups of democratic states, and there are few enough of those in existence or in prospect. It is a humble, imperfect, and fallible thing compared with the millenarian ideal. But it may just help to keep the peace while we wait.

EVERYDAY CONUNDRUMS: SOME PROBLEMS OF MICROMORALITY

*"What mighty contests rise from
trivial things."*
*—ALEXANDER POPE, "The Rape
of the Lock"*

▼

he grand moral choices of foreign policy are in a way the easiest to make. The need for decision can loom up suddenly and starkly, and the alternatives are quickly crystallized in national debate. But the choice can often be a false one: A glance beneath the surface of events or back over preceding years can often reveal that options have been narrowed to the point of preemption by a series of routine, more or less prudent, and more or less consciously made decisions. These daily concerns, the bread and butter of diplomacy, are worthy of greater attention than they receive.

At first sight what turn out to be considerable diplomatic problems may not even seem contentious. Rather, they can appear to be simple, self-contained issues whose resolution may not appear to involve matters of enormous moral significance. But like atoms, no sooner is each identified, than it can be broken down into infinite chains of smaller particles, each with its own individual ethical structure. At every stage, the element of casual expediency is there, as is the element of right and wrong. Attempts to disentangle the two can lead to a process of endless regression; like high energy particle physicists, we find ourselves peering at colliding particles as they break down into showers of new and intriguing quarks, from which we try to discern the ultimate constituents of moral matter.

Exact analysis of each inscrutable part of the whole becomes progressively more difficult the smaller it gets. It is, for example, far less easy than commonly supposed to identify what we think of as the element of simple expediency in a given decision. It is widely assumed that we all know instinctively what is good for us—what serves our interests best. But this is as untrue of diplomacy as it is of individual personalities. Before self-interest can conflict with morality, there must be some clear definition of the two. By isolating and analyzing some of the main elements that are likely to enter into routine decisions on arms sales, immigration, or foreign aid, we can quickly see that it can sometimes be as perplexing to decide what one *wants* to do as what one *ought* to do.

FOREIGN ARMS SALE

The sale of defense equipment is a notoriously emotive subject. Confronted with a decision on whether or not to sell an individual item to a particular country, at a particular moment, most of us would initially feel confident in our own seat-of-the-pants judgment. But if we are honest with ourselves, we will recognize that such judgments owe a good deal not only to utilitarian calculations of gain and loss but to preconceptions about the whole principle of arms deals and distinctions among different weapons, as well as to instinctive prejudice about the political attractiveness or otherwise of the country in question.

Any attempt at the deconstruction of the ethics of an individual sale must start from some basic view on the moral propriety of the export of arms. There are strongly conflicting attitudes that need to be resolved. One extreme view is that all arms sales, to whatever country and at whatever level of sophistication, are wrong. Even if they do not fuel the global arms race, they can nourish or stimulate local conflict. If everyone stopped selling arms to the Third World and the temptation of intervention by the great powers in local disputes were reduced as a consequence, the result would be a dramatic reduction in casualties and maybe in international tensions, even if some states made some themselves or resorted to more primitive weapons to pursue their feuds. An opposing view is that it is immoral to deprive smaller or weaker countries of the fundamental right of self-defense, enjoyed by all larger states and even neutral countries such as Sweden. A country that has no national manufacturing capability to produce what it decides it needs to protect itself should be allowed to arm itself in the international market-place. Otherwise, in practice, we are confining the right of self-protection to developed countries, thereby making weak countries weaker in the crucial area of their own security and hence an easier prey to pressures from larger and more powerful states. It can even be argued that denying arms to poor countries is a *de facto* form of imperialism, or of culpable stupidity if the country in question fell under the sway of a Communist power, say, as a result.

The major point of principle would be unlikely to be resolved in any final sense; no one would be likely to favor either selling everything to everyone or nothing to anyone. If the decision were made to proceed with the sale in question, those making it would in practice probably consult a list, preestablished for the purpose, differentiating broadly but not finally among classes of weapons that could be sold to different countries. The list itself would incorporate questionable distinctions and could be open to strong challenge on any number of grounds if it were publicly available. It could be kept up to date to reflect any changes in classes or sophistication of weaponry or in the situation on the ground—e.g., in the regime in the country in question. It would also need to record which other countries were capable and willing to supply particular weapons. In many cases, the resulting political and military permutations involved would be highly complex and subjective.

Suppose there had been a recent deterioration in the human rights record in a customer country—not yet to the point where it had been removed from the list for all manner of weapons but certainly to a point where the supply of any weapons that could be used for internal repression rather than external self-defense could provoke a strong public reaction in the selling country and internationally as well as possible friction between the supplying country and the neighbors of the customer. When subjected to an actual test of whether or not to supply, previously established distinctions among weapons categorized as offensive, non-offensive, or unlikely to be of any use for intimidation, crowd control, or against internal dissidents begin to look less clear. In the real world this probably means a dispute between the Ministry of Defense and the Foreign Ministry of the supplier country: The first regards the weapon as a fairly standard item of equipment; the diplomats, on the other hand, might see it as a minor but sophisticated piece of gear whose sale would be noticed by friends, neighbors, and adversaries alike. In present conditions the press would probably harp on any dual use—internal and external—

and perhaps see the sale as a deliberate act of policy, a signal aimed at influencing events in a particular direction. Further, as technical judgments shift, so the moral landscape would change with them. There are certain defined parameters: Many would agree that a submarine can be sold to a friendly or potentially friendly country that has a rather repressive regime but that CS gas for riot control cannot. There is, however, a great deal in between.

Matters could be infinitely more complex. The fact that the country in question is asking for the equipment may not mean that it needs it. The equipment may be a new gadget that has caught the fancy of the president or a general; worse still, the president himself may be a general. It may well languish in some warehouse, as other weapons sold to the country have in the past, and never be used or even maintained at all. This would presumably reduce the moral disincentive to selling.

Adding to the complexities for consideration, the country might be hideously overspending on arms and underspending on agriculture, in which case it would be neither ethical nor sensible to encourage such behavior. It must be in the longer term self-interest of the supplier country not only to stabilize a basically friendly regime but to build up the economy of the buying country and help it to develop as a trading partner. But then what is the point of refusing if we know perfectly well that a third country, less scrupulous than our own, will quickly step in and do a deal if we don't? We shall be left with intact principles, no contract, and reduced means of influencing things in a sensible direction.

More seriously, if the country has a persuasive case for acquiring the item, the local balance of power could be adversely affected if we failed to provide it. Of course, it would be far more sensible for the country to get together with its neighbors to sort out their differences, which may be as much personal and traditional as anything else. We have been trying for years to encourage them to do just that. But the fact is that they won't. Neighboring countries are being supplied with equivalent material by Communist states, who are thereby building up their influence in the region. A clear hint may have been dropped that if we don't supply, the Communists will.

Alternatively, the boot may be on the other foot. The buying country may be seeking to free itself from Communist influence, in part by diversifying its sources of arms supplies. The country is still at arm's length at the moment; but if we show ourselves willing in this instance, our sale could give us a toehold, and we could build on the resulting goodwill to wean it back closer to the democratic camp.

Besides the obvious political advantages, new civilian commercial opportunities could follow an arms sale. Conversely, failure to supply could jeopardize other contracts, some of which may be in the offing or the pipeline: We know that these matters are not decided on purely commercial grounds, but to some extent by the personal whim of a president, who might take a negative decision on the arms issue very badly.

But even if we sell, what are the chances of getting paid? The regime is already having talks with the International Monetary Fund. What is the point of entering a political minefield if we get the contracts but spend years thereafter wrangling about the cash?

Yet do we really have a choice at all, given the unemployment rate at home in the area where the defense industry in question is located? This order alone will keep three hundred men off the streets for three years, in a period of recession. The chances of the sale doing lasting damage to the client country or to the region or being used against its own civilian population begin to look slimmer when balanced against the certain domestic economic advantages. If the factory closes, the government will certainly lose the local seat at the next election.

Events are moving fast. If we don't decide soon, the

chance of a sale may disappear. If there is a leak while we prevaricate, we could end up getting all of the opprobrium and none of the benefits since the sale could be preempted by advance public criticism.

Yet can we be absolutely sure that the buyer country is seriously interested at all? All we have to go on is a single conversation at a diplomatic function between our military attaché and one of the president's advisers. Our man's grasp of the local language is good, but not infallible. The ambassador has backed the attaché, but then he always puts his weight behind anything that will "improve relations"— whatever that means—with his host country. Personnel says the attaché is enterprising but a little excitable, with a tendency to go native. There are also hints that he has problems with his wife, who thinks they have been out there too long. Maybe they have.

The purpose of this hypothetical case is to bring out the complexities of decision-making in such areas as defense sales, rather than to set up a model to which a key can be found. There can obviously be no clear-cut policy solution until the facts are clearly established—usually a far more untidy and less definitive business than is commonly supposed. Moreover some "facts" which could have a bearing on the morality or otherwise of the sale will depend heavily on subjective judgment. The final decision will thus be based as much on a balance of factual, as of ethical, uncertainties.

IMMIGRATION

There may be few overriding principles in foreign affairs, but one of them must surely be the humanitarian duty to help to resettle refugees, regardless of the difficulties in domestic terms. Let us imagine a particular group whose plight is pitiable; the television films of them risking life and limb to escape persecution in their own country are harrowing. Enormous pressure for decisive action is building up. But the government has an equally unqualified duty to see to the economic and social welfare of its own citizens. There are voices insisting that we have already done more than our fair share through aid and by accepting considerable numbers of refugees in the past. It is time that other countries did theirs.

The first thing to ascertain is the political situation on the ground in the country of origin. Are the refugees fleeing from anarchy or an uncontrollable civil war? Or are they being cynically encouraged to leave in the belief that someone somewhere will give them a home? If so, the more we take, the greater the pressure on others to leave will become. Would they really face persecution if they returned? It is hard to judge, especially since we have no representative in the country at the moment. Surely the first priority is to increase international pressure on the country to behave responsibly toward its own citizens? But effective international action against it is being blocked by a group of the country's friends at the United Nations. In any event, the country has passed the stage where appeals for more humane behavior mean much to its leaders—assuming they are still in control of events, given the signs of a power struggle in the government.

It could be claimed that we are under strong "moral" pressure to take the lead in this case, since the refugees come from an area that has close historical ties with our country. Conversely, there may be a good "moral" case for our taking a back seat, since they are clearly in the former sphere of interest of another country.

What are the Communist countries doing to help? Of course, the last thing the refugees want is to live in a Communist state, but at least the Communist countries should be encouraged to bring pressure on the regime to behave more responsibly and to contribute in cash and kind to the solution of the refugee problem. Why should the West always be expected to sweep up the mess?

More immigrants, from wherever they come, mean more trouble. We have enough domestic difficulty with racial tension already. "Only a few thousand more," we are told. But we know from experience that relatives will follow and that we will be seen as a soft touch. There is a wave of sympathy for the refugees now. But it will turn the other way the next time we have hot weather and a riot or two.

If these refugees are let in, we will come under immediate pressure to relax controls on others, who have a far better claim in terms of traditional ties with this country. Once the refugees are here, they will be an economic and social burden quite disproportionate to their numbers. In a recession, there is not a hope of getting them jobs: They don't even speak the language. Some may spend their time feuding and plotting against the regime in their home country. There could be a terrorist risk.

It is perfectly clear that, if we hold out against taking large numbers, countries with far less acute population pressures than ours will be forced to abandon their discriminatory immigration policies. But it is a slow process, and it would sound cynical to say that in public; while we wait, the clamor for action will increase.

In the last resort, all these factors are beside the point. There is no practical alternative to taking a sizable number immediately, come what may. There is an election soon, and we cannot go into it with those pictures still appearing on television while we do nothing about it. Let them in. It will satisfy all the emotions and the high-minded principles today. The electorate can repent at leisure.

Immigration is an even more emotive subject than arms sales, and the pressures for instant, unreflective action by governments will be all the more intense, although the long-term consequences of the decisions—the repercussions on host societies—will clearly be greater. Thus even a moral issue which at first sight would appear to be one that could be decided "straight from the heart" turns out to be less easy to resolve when its implications are laid bare.

FOREIGN AID

Economic aid to poor countries, it is often argued, is not charity but a moral duty. It seems completely indefensible that the gap between rich and poor should be so wide and growing. If the international community as a whole will not live up to its responsibilities, our country should give a lead by trebling the share of our gross national product we devote to aid, regardless of what the others decide. If they do not respond immediately, we will continue to seek to persuade them. Meanwhile we will go it alone and act by moral example.

Even with tripled funds, it is beyond the means of the richest countries to do anything significant for all those who need help. So we have to make a highly selective choice. Which are the countries in most urgent need? At first, the choice seems clear: There are countries where people are starving. But even there, how much should go into the immediate relief of starvation and how much into longer term aid? There are those who will argue, not unpersuasively, that the greatest good we can do is to encourage self-help: There is no future for a country that becomes reliant on others to feed its people, and no one will feed it forever.

All this assumes a cooperative, efficient, and reasonably stable government; otherwise the immediate relief will not get through, and the government will be unwilling or unable to plan improvements. The one thing the donor country cannot do—though the public seems to imagine otherwise—is to administer the country in question. Some of the immediate aid may stick to the hands of corrupt officials and be sold in the towns before it gets anywhere near those who need it. Agricultural reconstruction may be impeded by a host of factors—war, tradition, incompetence, lack of administrative infrastructure. No amount of virtuous intent will cut through this. There may be a war in progress or impending, which will hamper the distribution of aid and involve us in harsh decisions. Are we going to find ourselves feeding an army or feeding insurgents?

Maybe it is unwise to concentrate aid on hopelessly poor places? In terms of the greatest happiness of the greatest number, it could make sense to devote at least as much of one's energies and money to countries that are not the most indigent but that have the greatest promise for swift progress—that is, where a quicker and better return for aid can be expected and where, as it happens, the governments are also politically friendlier to the donor. The prospects for legitimate economic returns in the form of trade may well be far rosier there too; thus there could be a chance to give more help to a larger number of people for a longer period, while simultaneously benefiting the donor country, either by tied aid or the generation of mutual trade.

Important domestic political angles are involved. There could well be resentment that aid was being given to an ideologically unattractive regime, however needy, which could be fanned by reports of its being siphoned off for personal or political ends or by fears that aid was being used indirectly to strengthen the country's military potential by releasing funds for arms procurement—possibly from Communist states.

In every case, including the few instances where we face the most terrible spectacles of mass starvation, difficult ethical choices are present at every step. Giving practical expression to our nation's altruistic instincts is less easy than many suppose. Maybe we should just channel the money through one of the international aid organizations? Then we would get the moral benefits and leave the political judgments to people who may be least qualified to make them. But why is our government involved at all? Surely the purest form of aid comes from the individual conscience. The whole attempt to establish a national "aid budget" is artificial: How can there ever be a "correct" level? What we need are more generous tax incentives to encourage private donations to good causes. International aid, like domestic charity, should not depend on the proxy beneficence of governments.

Of the three problems briefly presented here that of aid has been most frequently and most thoroughly discussed in public. The major difference with the immigration issue is of course that we are dealing essentially with the future of other societies rather than our own. This is not to underestimate the interaction between Third World and Western economies. But it does mean that the ethical implications are more onerous for the decision-takers. A surge of ill-targeted generosity may provide the maximum degree of immediate moral self-gratification for the donor and the minimum of long-term benefit to the recipient.

All three problems—arms, immigration, and aid—have one thing in common. When seen not just through the long-sighted lens of the moral critic but through the action-oriented eyes of the practitioner of politics or diplomacy the problems are not—as is often imagined—simplified, but magnified. As we have noted, David Hume's view was that "the more we habituate ourselves to an accurate scrutiny of morals, the more delicate feeling do we acquire of the most minute distinctions between vice and virtue." When the object of the study is action rather than contemplation inherent dilemmas become entwined in an almost intractable ethical intricacy. While it would be wrong to ignore them, there comes a point where these intricacies have to be cut through with the knife of decision in ways that will inevitably sometimes seem arbitrary or hazardous, if there is going to be any action at all.

9

THE
ULTIMATE
MORALISM

*It is wrong to see malign
intentions in whole groups of men
and social classes. . . . You
[socialists] are misinterpreting
the moral categories of social life,
and at the same time, you are
completely denying the
responsibility of the human
personality. This combination of
extreme moralism and complete
immorality creates an unhealthy
spiritual atmosphere.*
—*NICHOLAS BERDYAEV,* On
Inequality

▼

Time and again in the nuclear debate, we are struck by a
sense of disproportion: Between the huge size of the arsenals on each side in relation to the destructive power of each
individual warhead; between the difficulty of defining the
Soviet threat in any immediate terms and the instant and
all-consuming means of retribution; and above all between
the extremes of technical refinement of the weapons themselves and the primitivism that characterizes so much of the
discussion about their use.

That man's technical prowess has outgrown his moral
stature is an unhelpful truism. But nowhere is the gap

wider or its implications more stark than in the matter of nuclear weapons. The dangers of moralism are starker here too.

Technology itself, the scientist assures us, is neutral, morally inert; it is a force for good or evil. In our daily lives this seems clear enough: Technology is there to be used or misused. Yet in the case of nuclear weapons the very extremes of power involved—this is not just a piece of applied science but the means of destroying most of civilization—strains our ability to regard them as a mere technical device like any other. Their devastating potential also makes nuclear weapons a vehicle for romantic attitudes—themselves a close cousin to moralistic frames of mind.

Romanticism has many connotations. Irving Babbitt draws a persuasive parallel between two of its incarnations: In a certain type of scientist whose lust for knowledge is untramelled by and unsubordinated to humane considerations; and in the self-centered, emotionally lustful Rousseauist whose true humanity—in the sense of his ability to think about others as well as feel about himself—is similarly in doubt.

As a literary movement romanticism has roots in medieval romances, a main ingredient of which was the superhuman powers of the heroes—again for good or evil. The superhuman easily shades into the inhuman, and in nuclear armaments the two are inextricably mixed. This duality is reflected in the vocabulary used about them: Nuclear weapons have "fabulous" power, but their use would be "monstrous."

Romanticism is based on the unreal. There is something distinctly unreal about the size of modern missiles; there is also something mesmeric about their potential for vanquishing evil or holding it in check and—in a sinister way—about their capacity for making an end of everything. The most natural reaction to the appearance of any man, creature, or object with fabulous attributes is to run away.

The instinct to escape from the nuclear predicament is just as natural. But in a couple of easy strides, the giant will soon catch up.

Sincere, knowledgeable, and reflective men and women, overcome by the ethical enormity of the very possession of nuclear weapons, have advocated their unilateral abandonment. Others, equally certain of their ground, see them as agents of moral good: They prevent wars, deter aggression, and hold back the totalitarian tide. Quite apart from their strong views on the foolhardiness of one-sided nuclear disarmament, they find it genuinely difficult to conceive of a nuclear-free world that would be safer than the one we live in at present. In their most ideologically assertive mood, such people are prepared to respond to accusations of inhumanity by maintaining that they are the guardians of the only humanity worth preserving. To that extent, at their most extreme they can give an impression of being in thrall to nuclear weapons, captives of their magical powers for good. For them such weapons are a supreme talisman of freedom.

Rarely is the convergence of the Pietist and Brutalist modes of moral thinking more striking than in the nuclear field. Both share a "total" attitude, an urge for the absolute and a consequent intolerance for ambiguities or half-measures. On both sides too technology frequently comes to dominate moral thinking in subtle ways: It is the weapons themselves, their numbers, throwweight and all the rest that matters, rather than human agencies. And however strongly and genuinely the disarmer protests his concern for the future of mankind, both he and his Brutalist brother are in fact often at one in eliding the human factor from the equation. The natural consequence is that disarmers and nuclear crusaders pose an almost equivalent threat to world peace.

No sane person finds it difficult to sympathize with the motives of those who seek to remove the threat of nuclear war by simply abandoning on one side the means of conducting it in the hope that this will render nuclear war even more unthinkable, if not physically impossible. Such people are right to suppose that these weapons do pose immense moral problems. But they are wrong to refuse to see those problems in conventional ethical terms: That is, as questions requiring a solution that rests firmly on a moral tripod of aims, means, and consequences.

In the world as it is, what the disarmers are proposing is an unprecedented gesture of self-abnegation. A single giant would be left to roam the forest alone in the earnest hope that he would not run amuck or misuse his strength. Given what we know of his habits and the fallibility of human nature even under representative government—demonstrated in Hiroshima and Nagasaki—complete unilateral disarmament calls for a very considerable act of faith as well as abnegation.

One of the most distinctive factors in the disarmer's moral position is the urgency of his concern and the conviction that the only means of solving the problem is by a dramatic and, in essence, emotional act. The aim of ridding the world of nuclear weapons is not confined to one-sided disarmers. It is shared by many statesmen, who are prepared to justify their retention meanwhile on what they see as respectable moral grounds. The disarmers, by contrast, either distrust the process of nuclear negotiation or are impatient with it, fearing that a holocaust may overtake the world before multilateral disarmament can be achieved and that only the immediate renunciation of weapons by one side will preempt it.

A similar sense of urgency, tinged with the same romantic impatience with reality, can be felt among the most fervent Western proponents of nuclear superiority. They believe that unless the West keeps the Russians at bay by a massive array of armaments and a constant readiness to use them the Communists will strike and democratic society will perish. The terminology may seem a little excessive, but it is possible to detect in the arguments of both disarmers and nuclear supremacists the same eschatological overtones.

A second common characteristic of the Pietist and Brutalist approach to nuclear issues lies in their fascination, already noted, with the weapons themselves. It is not just that they are equally overawed by their potency; in the writings of the most articulate and scientifically astute partisans of disarmament, it is possible to discern a distinctive intellectual relish with the paradoxes and intricacies of nuclear strategy, the minutiae of missile accountancy, and the technical refinements of the weapons. It is curious and highly revealing to find the disarmers discussing with the same clinical detachment as some of their opponents the mathematics of survival. The point is nicely illustrated by the conversion of the anti-nuclear scientist, Jonathan Schell, into a passionate supporter of the Strategic Defense Initiative—another form of total, technical solution.

In the light of this mutual fixation with size, potency, and technique and with the search for immediate, comprehensive answers to complex ethical problems, it is logical that there should also be a close convergence in the underlying attitude of our nuclear moralists, whether abolitionists or militant retentionists, on the central question of the nature of the adversary and the relationship with the Russians themselves.

In his own estimation, the survival of humanity is the single, overriding ethical imperative that drives the nuclear disarmer. The aim is hardly in question; only a madman, a fanatic, or a cosmic misanthrope would contest the view that humanity is worth preserving. But the word "humanity" is richly ambiguous, signifying both humankind in the neutral sense and at the same time mankind at its most "humane," at its best. Disarmers rest too much of their case on this latter aspect, especially in their assessment of Soviet motives.

Both the nuclear enthusiast and the abolitionist are brothers under the skin, since both are unrealistic in their assessments of the Soviets. The first underrates the human capacity for good, by romanticizing the Communists' propensity for evil and by denying them any residual capacity for moral reasoning or even enlightened self-interest. In other words, he *dehumanizes* the adversary. In calculating the consequences of unilateralism, the disarmer, on the other hand, fails to take adequate account of the capacity for wickedness of humanity in general and of the Soviet regime in particular, thereby *dehumanizing* him in precisely the same way, but with the opposite result.

The political attitudes of those who favor unilateral nuclear disarmament towards the nature of Soviet society and the Soviet leadership are a relatively neglected area in the nuclear debate. It is sometimes too readily assumed that the partisans of one-sided disarmament must be partisans of, or at least sympathizers with, Soviet power. This confuses the disarmament movement of the post-war years—which was dominated or at least largely influenced by pro-Communists or simply Soviet stooges—with the more variegated patterns of nuclear protest in recent years. Today's anti-nuclear movement is influenced more by what it sees as ethical motives than by political ones. This does not make its prescriptions any safer—perhaps the contrary because it risks being that much more detached from the reality of politics. But it is neither intellectually just nor particularly helpful to label all disarmers as apologists for Moscow.

Indeed, the ethical concerns that lead many to question the West's nuclear policies are crucially similar in some respects to those of people whose main motivation in increasing the arms race is a visceral dislike of the Russians. Just as they share an impatience with diplomatic negotiations and the tortuousness of the arms control process, so they are reluctant to analyze rationally the dynamics of Soviet power and Soviet society. Both are therefore unclear about the possible consequences of their proposals, which are based more on their own subjective attitudes than on the objective evidence of developments in the Soviet Union itself.

The consequences of one-sided disarmament, though intrinsically difficult to predict, would clearly be manifold. Theoretically, they could include a nuclear attack by the adversary, though that seems neither the most likely nor the most immediate threat. The main and clearly foreseeable result of Western disarmament would be the weakening of the most "moral," or altruistic, element in American policy towards the Soviet Union: It would curtail the United States' ability not only to prevent global war by deterrence but to help to contain within certain limits (e.g., in the Gulf) the threat posed by the Soviet Union's expansionism abroad, while seeking the peaceful evolution of the Soviet regime over time towards a more liberal society. It is not clear how the achievement of any of these aims would be facilitated by giving the Russians a virtual monopoly on the world's most powerful weapons.

There is no obvious division between the non-nuclear and the nuclear, the local and the global. It is possible to foresee a train of events following one-sided nuclear disarmament that might begin with increased Soviet bullying of Poland and lead first to conventional war of unparalleled ferocity in Western Europe, then to Soviet nuclear threats against the United States itself.

It is not at all clear why it could be considered a more "moral" act to make the world safer for conventional war than to rely on nuclear weapons to maintain a workable peace. It would also be an action of unprecedented ethical egoism to allow the Russians to be in a position to threaten to use nuclear weapons against a Western or non-Western country following Western disarmament. Why should not the Soviet Union repeat Nagasaki? If Americans were capable of dropping the bomb on Japan from good motives, why should not the Russians at least threaten to do the same from bad ones? None of the proponents of one-sided disarmament have provided satisfactory replies. For the West to clear its conscience at the expense of others would hardly be a moral act. It would, in fact, be an act of ethical inversion— another typical manifestation of moralism. As Rousseau said of Mme. de Warens, "Her conduct was reprehensible, but her heart was pure" *(Confessions)*.

Nuclear enthusiasts in America and Europe betray signs of a similarly introverted moral vision, being more concerned with the pursuit of the intellectual, national, and political feud with the Soviet Union and with their moral outrage at its very existence than with the nature of the country itself and its people or the wider effects of the policies they advocate. Perhaps the wisest remark on Soviet-U.S. relations was not about missiles or Afghanistan but about inner states of mind toward the adversary: George Kennan's warning against looking at the Soviet Union for a reflection of your own virtue. This is a way of saying that moralism feeds on the iniquities of others.

The United States' foreign policy is strongly influenced by a dual reliance on technical efficiency and ethical assertion; it has the power to impose the "right" solutions and a historical aversion to moral compromise. At its best, the tradition is the noble one of right enforced by might. At its worst, it can relapse into an unstable mixture of technological and moralistic vehemence.

There is no clearer example of the foreign policy consequences of these attitudes than in some recent episodes of the superpower relationship with the Soviet Union. We may now be emerging into calmer waters, but that in itself makes it worth reflecting for a moment on what we have come through and why. Western leaders are fond of stressing that nuclear weapons alone do not cause war. We should, then, pay at least as much attention to the politics as to the weapons. But at some points in the recent past, not only has defense come to dominate the West's stance towards Moscow, but the politics have become more atavistic as the weapons have multiplied in power and sophistication. The United States has portrayed the Soviet Union not just as a repressive society with an expansionist ideology but as "evil" and posing an immediate threat to world peace, a threat that had to be met by forceful new countermeasures. Any attempt to shade the picture was seen as evidence of moral inertia and immoral predilection for compromise, or something even worse.

One of the clearest warning signals that something was wrong with this view of the Soviets was that basic, everyday truths of human behavior were held not to embrace the Russians; in Moscow only single motivations were deemed to apply. Thus, while everyone agrees that the Soviet Union is guilty of aggressive attitudes and actions (e.g., in Afghanistan or Poland), there was reluctance to accept the obvious truth, for which there is abundant historical as well as contemporary evidence, that, in acting in this way, the Russians may also be motivated in some degree by insecurity, for example, by the threat of Islamic fundamentalism seeping into the Soviet Union through its southern flank. That aggressiveness and insecurity are two sides of the same coin is a banal enough comment on daily life; but when applied to Soviet foreign policy, it was unacceptable to nuclear moralists.

To deal with such an infinity of wickedness, we were told, only superior might would suffice. Here again, no ambiguity was permitted; any talk of a balance of power with such a sinister opponent would itself be immoral. Hence too the "window of opportunity" mentality: The conviction that the Kremlin was permanently poised to strike and that we must base our calculations on their determination to act on the remotest pretext. That there may well be weaknesses in the West's defenses that needed repair is undeniable. But the assumption that the Russians have the intent as well as the capability to exploit them as soon as they appear confuses means and motives—another symptom of the moralistic approach.

A further characteristic of the nuclear extremist is the dramatization of the strengths of the adversary and of one's own deficiencies. "Window of opportunity" adherents dwell in frightening detail on any loophole in the West's defenses, no matter how theoretical. But they fail to consider how life must have looked from Moscow when it was faced with the imminent disintegration of Soviet control over Poland, which created in the eyes of some of its leaders at least a theoretical "corridor of opportunity" for the West. Since Poland was a channel for Western "liberal" ideas under the czars and for German invasions in two world wars, its slide towards the West may have looked a less abstract "threat" to a regime with some reason to feel nervous about its own population.

From such gladiatorial attitudes flowed the almost supernatural reliance on the technology of defense to exorcise the Soviet evil. The Soviet Union was seen as a red version of the Green Knight: A single beheading would not suffice if another would instantly grow in its place. Negotiation was pointless too: Once the adversary was firmly characterized as "inhuman," there was little to be gained by contact with him and much to be lost. Diplomacy itself, with its overtones of conciliation, became unethical.

So it was that in 1983, a year of severe superpower tensions, while intermediate range missiles were being installed in Europe in response to the Soviet deployment of SS20's, intergovernmental intercourse reached a new and, in retrospect, unnecessary low. In terms of human contact, the two main American visitors to Moscow in that year were a ninety-two-year-old veteran diplomat, Averill Harriman, and a twelve-year-old girl on a sentimental peace mission.

The decline in official contacts with the Russians was matched by an ever-increasing emphasis on the role of weaponry in the East-West relationship. The less we knew or wanted to know at first hand about Soviet society, politicians, or generals, the more fixated we became on their weapons and our own. The decline in the study of *homo russicus* was neatly paralleled by the rise of strategic studies.

Whole areas of East-West relations began to be dominated by a sort of strategic sociology, a science of nuclear behaviorism. Like most pseudosciences it was characterized by over-reliance on statistics and a relentless emphasis on the mechanical margin to the exclusion of everything else. Like most bad sociology too the statistics deployed to prove the case were often skewed by partisanship from the start.

So the two pillars of nuclear moralism were in place: A strategy of total superiority, powered by strong feeling. There was not room for two giants in the forest, and we felt we had to be ready at every instant to burn it down—trees, birds, and all—to prevail over the other one.

Inevitably, now that the tensions have subsided, it will be argued—*post hoc, ergo propter hoc*—that such a dramatization was the only way to soften the Russians' resistance to real negotiation. This is historically untrue and a rather obvious piece of latter-day rationalization. Looking back a few years, one's feelings are more like those of a person who has escaped a possible mishap because of someone else's bad driving: The more one realizes that the risk, however slight, need never have occurred, the more one's relief is mixed with retrospective indignation. In the case of East-West relations, moreover, the consequences of these excesses will not be easily overcome. Real damage has been done to the West's diplomatic position in the meantime. One of the worst effects has been a new tendency among ordinary people to ask whether there was really a Soviet threat at all? People heard much about its imminence, but they did not see it. They were told we were weak, but they paid through high taxes for a steady accumulation of weapons of gigantic destructive power and an overwhelmingly deterrent effect. At the same time they were insistently reminded of the inherent fragility of the Soviet economy and Soviet society. For the man in the street, it must have all been very puzzling.

Out of this confusion there arose a new debate about the nature of Soviet power, which resolved little, merely taking us back to all the old uncertainties. Once again we wondered whether we preferred our Russians "thin" or "fat"—whether they were more dangerous in poverty or prosperity—and consequently whether we should trade with them and, if so, in what. The illusion here is that in a capitalist society, except in the case of sensitive items, there is not a great deal of choice in what is traded (another example of trying to detach domestic realities from foreign policy). Nor does it make a great deal of difference to the Soviet Union in the long term. The debate on trade still continues, but it is unlikely to influence Soviet development one way or the other, except at the margin and in the eyes of those who dwell on the importance of the margin.

Next, we sought to decide whether the Russians were as aggressive as they seemed. Again, the answer was as inconclusive as it has always been. And finally, we tried fruitlessly to disentangle national from ideological motives: To discover whether the Russians misbehaved because they were Russians or because they were Communists. In any other walk of life this might not seem a very profitable enquiry, given that the outcome would necessarily be unclear and not susceptible to proof. And so it proved to be. Needless to say, this sterile and exhausting argument left the Russians largely as they were before.

But such extremes of moralistic fervor can produce un-expected results. Ordinary, sensible people dislike living on their nerves, and when the reaction comes, it is easy to get caught up in the relief from tension and to ask what it was all for? But it is not just the man in the street who asks himself this question: Diplomats and statesmen are not im-mune from such emotional reactions.

Some years ago, after his first meeting with Chou En-lai, the former Chinese Prime Minister, after the long Sino-American estrangement, a very senior American (not Dr. Kissinger) cried. He was presumably overcome less by the historic significance of the moment than by the contrast be-tween the "yellow peril" image of the Chinese leadership so widely accepted in the West and the civilized, intelligent, and occasionally charming original in the form of Chou. Not surprisingly, Chou's undoubted ruthlessness was not on show at the time of the meeting.

It seems unlikely that many people will respond quite so emotionally to Mikhail Gorbachev, though the same ten-dency to overreact to unsuspected intimations of humanity have been evident. Sentimentalism, romanticism, and mor-alism are closely related. Once the central balance of things is so powerfully disrupted by alternate bouts of "hard" and "soft" emotionalism, it is hard to regain stability: In this case, the stability of a soundly based consensus for defense in the United States and in European countries, and in the Atlantic Alliance as a whole. Irrational anti-Sovietism and an emotional yearning for peace at any price are powerful potions. It will take time to clear them from the system.

Against this background, it is entirely predictable that there should now be so much heady talk by statesmen about doing away altogether with nuclear weapons in a relatively short time. It would be foolish to deny that new oppor-tunities have grown with the arrival of Gorbachev. But this makes it all the more important not to ricochet from an extreme of pessimism to imprudent optimism.

Assuming a willingness on our own side to bring the level of weapons down and eventually to eliminate them, two other factors are essential: One is some reasonable assurance of continuity of Soviet policy—and it would be rash to stake too much on one man's personality in a country with a history of untimely disappearances among its leaders. The other is that we need some reassurance that the greater predisposition to conflict, which is endemic in non-democratic regimes, will subside together with nuclear arsenals. Otherwise there is the stark risk of making the world ready for conventional war, beginning in Europe.

Because we are talking about the gradual democratization of the Soviet Union itself, we are looking at a long period during which nuclear weapons are likely to continue to exist at some levels. It is therefore wrong and "moralistic" to lead the public to believe otherwise; to open up visions of nuclear-free stability before the substance is there to underpin the aspirations. Hence the widespread apprehension and confusion at the outcome of the Reykjavik summit.

To be fair, the American government has always made clear its eventual aim of freeing the planet from the nuclear threat. What other governments—and some Americans—find unnerving is the speed of the transition in Washington from an attitude of absolute mistrust of the Soviet adversary to one of readiness to join with Moscow in the eradication of all weapons of mass destruction within a historically abrupt timescale. To many it seemed that America was about to lurch from a strategy of nuclear-based security to a millenarian vision of a nuclear-free future. However welcome the change of emphasis, it seems to have more to do with sentiment than strategy as the pendulum of moralism swung from stormy to bright.

By their very nature, nuclear weapons pose an ethical problem for which there is no direct precedent. But the weapons are man-made, and only a morality anchored in the reality of human experience and the wisdom distilled from that experience will prevent their use. Opposite and interacting forms of moralism combine in practice to make their use marginally more likely.

Just as we have no ready-made system of morals to apply to our daily lives or to the routine conduct of governments, still less do we have any clear ethical framework to accommodate the assault on our consciences that must be posed by the existence of such weapons. It is sometimes tempting though not very helpful to see their very presence as evidence of the bankruptcy of all ethical systems and of man's moral will.

For centuries churchmen, scholars, and soldiers have discussed just and unjust wars. But the relevance of that debate itself is now in question, if only because there could be no more precedents to analyze after a nuclear exchange and no further opportunity to learn from experience. The rules of warfare, as they have evolved over the centuries, are only partially applicable. When it comes to nuclear weapons, we are driven back to more fundamental principles.

The first and most pressing need is to reestablish the human dimension: In the real world there are brigands, but no giants in the forest. To regain this sense of *terra firma* we are driven back to Aristotle. Bertrand Russell wrote irritably of him that "there is not a word that rises above commonsense in his ethical theories" (*A History of Human Philosophy*, p. 191). We can see why Russell, with his antinomian temperament, found this so exasperating. But Russell was also a vigorous opponent of nuclear weapons in his later years. If he were alive today, he might welcome a little dull sobriety to alleviate the nuclear enervation from which we have seemed to suffer in recent years and grudgingly admit that there is still room for Aristotle's common sense in international affairs.

Reading Aristotle, the practitioner of foreign policy is reminded of the inextricability of virtuous action and practical action, of morality and the facts. Nuclear weapons exist. They will continue to exist, perhaps in the hands of countries with less circumspect leaderships than that of the Soviet Union, whether the West keeps or abandons its own. Clearly, such "facts of life" must not be confused with the whole moral reality and paralyze the moral will. But there can be no effective exertion of this will if it fails to take account of them.

The second Aristotelian premise that directly impinges on the nuclear dilemma is the need for the avoidance of extravagance in all its forms. This points immediately to the dangers of the unnecessary stockpiling of weapons. But here the argument needs refinement. Paradoxically, Aristotle is unlikely to have been a partisan of the "freeze" movement, or even an automatic adherent of proposals to cut arsenals by an arbitrary percentage. He saw clearly enough that balance may involve asymmetry and illustrated the point in a peculiarly apposite image when he wrote:

> *It is a matter of avoiding too much and too little, and what is right for one might not be right for another . . . for instance, if ten is many and two is few, six is the intermediate, taken in terms of the object, for it exceeds and is exceeded by an equal amount. This is intermediate according to arithmetical proportions. But the intermediate relatively to us is not to be taken so. If ten pounds are too much for a particular person to eat, and two too little, it does not follow that the trainer will order six pounds, for this also is perhaps too much for the person who is to take it, or too little—too little for Milo* [a famous wrestler], *too much for the beginner in athletic exercises* (Nicomachean Ethics, *p. 100).*

In nuclear terms, how can such needs be defined? Obviously in part by the physical strength of the potential adversary. But in calculating this, the central rule of eschewing excess, which may mean abandoning the search for exact "equivalence," must also apply. The same is true of the conduct of the political relationship with Moscow. The cultivation of exaggerated apprehension about Soviet intentions or the dramatization of one's own vulnerability would be immoral. So would unbridled rhetoric in public exchanges with the Russians, which itself would feed such fears. Undue reliance on the defense relationship to the exclusion of political, cultural, or other ties would also fall foul of Aristotelian ethics, especially since such an emphasis would also lead to a further stimulation to inordinate levels of armaments and tensions. "Tit for tat" reactions to Soviet behavior, though sometimes justified, also tend to imply a false moral equivalence between democratic and coercive regimes.

But excess has at least two sides: It would be equally wrong to indulge in misplaced trustfulness or sentimentalism in relations with the Russians, especially while their "wrestlers'—the military—continue to be fed on gargantuan diets.

Kant too, as we have seen, would have disapproved of the endless accumulation of armaments; he was already concerned in his own day by the growth of military budgets, glumly observing that "the cost of peace finally becomes more oppressive than that of a short war" *(Perpetual Peace,* p. 5). But the mere establishment of a tolerable balance to reduce the risks of war, which might have satisfied Aristotle, would not have been enough for him. Always alert against moral relativism, he might have objected to the idea that the stability of the East-West relationship and the security of the West should continue indefinitely to be based on weapons capable of annihilating humanity itself. Today, such misgivings are not confined to one-sided disarmers but are shared by some NATO strategists too. The feeling that there is something inherently wrong in nuclear weapons themselves is implicitly recognized in the declarations of intent on disarmament by both Western and Soviet governments, even when these appear to be largely a matter of form.

It is this emphasis on the centrality of mankind as an aim in itself and his concern with the moral will that continue to assure the German philosopher of a voice in today's nuclear debate. It is true that the language of moral imperatives can become a double-edged sword, which both Pietists and Brutalists can attempt to wield to their separate advantage. The same writer who insisted that humanity is an end in itself also wrote that it was essential to do what is right even though the whole world should perish. But the most sober interpretation of the latter view is surely that Kant was using a figure of speech that has acquired a literalism he could not have anticipated. No similar ambiguity attaches to his main doctrine: "So act that you can will that your maxim could become a universal law, regardless of the end" *(Perpetual Peace,* p. 42). Given the danger of nuclear proliferation, there seems no obvious means of reconciling this maxim with the indefinite reliance on nuclear weapons for our security or encouraging others to do the same.

As we have seen, the doctrines of the utilitarian school of ethics fit all too conveniently with some current political attitudes to nuclear weapons: The greatest security of the greatest number is thought by most Western governments to rest on the maintenance of the deterrent. But this does not deal with the question of the morality or otherwise of their ownership. Perhaps the clearest modern synthesis of the lessons of Aristotle, Kant, and Bentham was Pope John Paul's statement a few years ago that nuclear weapons are only morally tolerable so long as we are genuinely striving to dispose of them (Message from Pope John Paul II to the General Assembly of the United Nations, 1982).

CONCLUSION

> *. . . a degree of familiarity with*
> *history . . . is our only available*
> *source of an ethical education . . .*
> —*JOSEPH BRODSKY, "A Cambridge*
> *Education"*

▼

We were warned by philosophers themselves that ethics is a difficult subject. Hunting down moralistic heresies in international affairs has taken us through large expanses of variegated countryside, far removed, it may seem, from the well-trodden paths of the perennial foreign policy debate. But these are not mere speculative by-ways; they are remote from the foreign policy process only in the same sense as the spreading roots are remote from the stability of the tree.

Yet even if we may have succeeded in tracking down some pernicious practices and attitudes, we seem no nearer to a definition of what constitutes a clear moral framework of international relationships in the conditions of a late twentieth-century democracy, let alone how the issues of the day sit within it.

A glance at the contemporary debate suggests that all that is really needed is more "openness" in the formulation of policy. There are clearly times when concealment or excessive secrecy are immoral in themselves and openness wise as well as healthier. But to assume that adjustments in bureaucratic practice to release more "information" to the public will of themselves produce a more moral and less devious foreign policy is a comforting fallacy. It may help. But the notion that the public is straining toward virtue in its dealings with foreigners and that all it needs is an improved supply of facts or confidences is an appealing but essentially sentimental fiction. It is a harmful fiction too insofar as it reinforces the equally attractive illusion that foreign policy is made by governments and that the media, the intellectuals, and the public are mere critics, detached or deliberately excluded from the action and its ethical consequences. That seems far too comfortable a posture for all concerned, not least governments themselves.

"Open government" happens to be high on the political agenda in the 1980s and one of the most topical moral issues at the moment. But that does not make it *the* or even *a* fundamental problem. Societies, like individuals, are in the habit of evading fundamental problems if they possibly can, and of inflating pseudo-problems to the maximum possible extent to disguise the evasion. What is really needed is something far less mechanistic and far more exacting than more "information": A new morality of public responsibility in foreign affairs. For that more openness is a necessary but by no means a determining precondition.

Fine words, which need to be tethered firmly to the ground if they are not to drift away to mingle with the circumambient gas that surrounds the whole subject of morality. The firmest and most fertile ground available is in the field of education. Here again scope for cynicism is not lacking: If the realization of the centuries-old ideal of "education for democratic citizenship" has been less than spectacular at home, can anything be done to prepare for the exercise of responsible moral choice in the special field of foreign affairs?

If, as this book began by noting, our leaders are less and less likely themselves to have the leisure or inclination to sharpen their moral awareness by reflecting on the niceties of ethical judgments or by probing the philosophical basis of these judgments, to expect any great part of the electorate to pursue this standard of awareness would be a pious hope indeed. Nor would it be realistic to think in terms of more formal education for the exercise of democratic responsibilities in foreign affairs. Strange things feature on today's educational timetable, but the morality of international relations has not yet reached the status of what the educationalists call a "specialism." It would be a bold man who drew up the curriculum.

In any event, "moral education," for whatever purpose, does not necessarily depend on formal schooling at all but on such values as restraint and altruism that can be and are nurtured outside the classroom as the products of daily experience and individual moral effort. All this can be highly relevant to foreign policy: In the politics of defense, for example, there is a central place for common-sense ethics, wherever and however those qualities are imbibed.

But it by no means follows that schools have no place in the development of a more ethically aware electorate. What happens in the classroom can powerfully affect adult attitudes and judgments, often for the worse. At present, from the narrow viewpoint of foreign policy ethics, it is hard to imagine a less propitious climate than that which appears to prevail in current educational practice. Two broad concepts seem to dominate: Vocationalism, which today means science and technology, and self-expression. These two elements can and do combine to induce children into ways of thinking that are the worst possible preparation for responsible moral choice in a nuclear age. Together they can form a heady mixture of scientific determinism and emotional self-indulgence: The main constituents, as it happens, of nuclear moralism. The gaunt grammar of technology is replacing that of language and true communication, untempered by a broader or deeper humanistic culture and inflamed by untutored and unrestrained self-assertion.

The situation is not necessarily improved and can indeed be further aggravated by misguided attempts to make what the pupil learns about the world more "relevant" to what he sees and hears outside the classroom. Sometimes this takes the form of seeking to broaden a child's understanding by reference to "current affairs." Still worse, it can take the form of the deeply misconceived notion of "peace studies." In practice both are likely to reinforce the relentlessly one-dimensional emphasis on the contemporary and on the reactive emotionalism stimulated by the excitable news bulletins of the electronic media. The only time that the average child can hope to be abstracted from all this is the time spent in the classroom. If that brief detachment from the pressures of the everyday is removed from him, he will be the more likely to turn into a prefabricated social unit, reproducing and regurgitating the second-hand analyses of the day with a terrifying sense of personal conviction, as if he had discovered them himself.

In the matter of defense, instead of looking to himself to make sane, ethical judgments, based on some minimal awareness of past experience, the pupil is more likely to learn the patois of "rights" rather than of obligations, including of course the fundamental "right" to peace. Alternatively, his uneducated, unhistorical young mind may be captivated by notions of nuclear virility: The counting of warheads and the cultivation of strong feelings about the

Russians. Either way, as constituted at present, many of our schools on both sides of the Atlantic seem well geared to the production of a plentiful supply of Pietists and Brutalists for the future.

What seems most obviously lacking in our present approach to education is the very quality that is needed today in foreign policy more than in any other political sphere and more than in any other epoch: A simple, classical sense of perspective, and hence of proportion. This depends crucially on a sense of the past. It ought not to be too much to ask of the costly apparatus of universal education, which has been put into place since Kant's day, to convey to pupils of varying abilities some awareness of that past, however fragmentary, and of respect for, if not real understanding of the achievements of philosophers, writers, and historians. Yet we start from a position where, according to one recent survey two-thirds of American seventeen-year-olds do not know when the Civil War was fought, and half cannot identify Churchill or Stalin *(The New York Times,* April 20, 1987). It is not clear how well British children would perform in a similar survey.

The point is not to turn children away from present-day problems or from the economic necessities of life. It is rather a matter of finding ways to evoke through the reading of literature and history some glimmering of understanding of possible other worlds and so of historical and moral perspectives. If that sounds idealistic, it is worth remembering that we are after all dealing with a new generation of electors who by their choice of leaders will control weapons capable of obliterating the past, together with the future, simultaneously.

It may be foolish to seek to turn electors into intellectuals but not to educate voters to respect the intellect. Stalin, Hitler, and, in his last days, Mao were all surrounded by a number of uncultivated or even anti-intellectual mediocrities. In "The Coming Victory of Democracy," his still compelling speech delivered in America during his exile from Nazi Germany, Thomas Mann dwelt, like Kant, on the crucial relationship between peace, democracy, and education, saying, "because of its association and solidarity with knowledge, truth, justice, and as the opposite of violence and vulgarity, intellect becomes the advocate and representative of democracy on earth" (p. 38). He also argued that representative government and thus peace would only prevail if what he called democracy's "deep and forceful recollection of itself" and "the renewal of its spiritual and moral self-consciousness" (p. 61) were present within democratic countries. In much of our educational practice over recent decades it is precisely these qualities that have been eroded, together with the philosophical and historical understanding of the basis of democracy itself.

The British and Americans have been among the most enthusiastic in their assault on the values Mann was seeking to uphold. But none of this is unique to either Britain or America: A few years ago, President Mitterrand became so alarmed at the decline of history teaching in French schools that he issued a statement warning against the effects of collective amnesia, and called on the educational authorities to take remedial action. Obviously, the president was concerned as much with the preservation of France's sense of national identity as with the concept of moral self-improvement through the study of history. But the two do not necessarily conflict.

In the United States, a nuclear superpower, the implications of "collective amnesia" in any form, in the White House or the electorate, run deeper. George Santayana warned about the dangers of the "mechanized democrat" ("Americanism," p. 198), whose mind is innocent of any sense of the past and of the danger that those who do not remember history are condemned to repeat it. In the last quarter of the twentieth century, many episodes of history could be repeated only once.

BIBLIOGRAPHY

Aristotle. *The Nicomachean Ethics,* Penguin Classics, 1979.

Babbitt, Irving. *Rousseau and Romanticism,* University of Texas Press, 1977.

Bate, W. Jackson. *Samuel Johnson,* Harvest, 1979.

Baudelaire, Charles. *Intimate Journals,* Panther, London, 1969.

Bentham, Jeremy. *The Principles of Morals and Legislations, Ethical Theories,* ed. A.I. Melden, Prentice-Hall, 1967.

Berdyaev, Nicholas. *De L'Inégalité,* Editions L'Age d'Homme, 1976.

Boorstin, Daniel J. *The Americans,* Vintage Books, 1965.

Brodsky, Joseph. "A Cambridge Education," *Times Literary Supplement,* January 30, 1987.

Burke, Edmund. *Reflections on the French Revolution,* Pelican, 1968.

Butler, Bishop Joseph. *Fifteen Sermons, Ethical Theories,* Ed. A. I. Melden, Prentice-Hall, 1967.

Carlyle, Thomas. *The French Revolution,* Chapman and Hall, London, 1837.

Chapman, Guy. *The Dreyfus Trials,* Rupert Hart-Davis, 1955.

Dreiser, Theodore. *Dreiser Looks at Russia,* Constable, London, 1928.

Eliot, T.S. *Notes Towards The Definition of Culture,* Faber and Faber, 1962.

French, Peter. "Morally Blaming Whole Populations," *Philosophy, Morality and International Affairs,* Oxford University Press, 1974.

Gladstone, William. *The Bulgarian Horrors and the Question of the East,* John Murray, 1876.

Gu Cheng. "A Generation," *Mao's Harvest,* Oxford University Press, 1983.

Hampshire, Stuart. "Morality and Pessimism," *Public and Private Morality,* Cambridge University Press, 1978.

Heidegger, Martin. "Letter on Humanism," *Basic Writings,* Harper and Row, 1977.

—— "La Chose," *Essais et Conférences,* Gallimard, 1958.

Hobbes, Thomas. *Leviathan,* Pelican Classics, 1968.

Hoffman, Stanley. *Duties Beyond Borders,* Syracuse University Press, 1981.

Hume, David. *An Enquiry Concerning The Principles of Morals, Ethical Theories,* ed. A.I. Melden, Prentice-Hall, 1967.

Huxley, Aldous. *The Doors of Perception,* Chatto and Windus, 1954.

Jaspers, Karl. *Nietzsche,* Gateway, 1979.

Kant, Immanuel. *Foundations of The Metaphysics of Morals, Ethical Theories,* ed. A.I. Melden, Prentice-Hall, 1967.

—— *Idea For A Universal History,* Bobbs-Merrill, 1963.

—— *Perpetual Peace,* Bobbs-Merrill, 1957.

—— *Critique of Pure Reason,* Anchor Books, 1966.

Kennan, George. "The Gorbachev Prospect," *New York Review of Books,* January 21, 1988.

Lefever, Ernest W. "Moralism and U.S. Foreign Policy," *Orbis*, Summer 1972.

Macaulay, Thomas. "Defence of Mill," *Miscellaneous Writings,* Longman, Green, Longman, Roberts and Green, London, 1865.

Machiavelli, Niccolò. "The Art of War," *The Chief Works and Others,* Duke University Press, 1965.

——*The Prince.*

——*The Discourses.*

Mann, Thomas. *The Coming Victory of Democracy,* Secker and Warburg, 1938.

Mill, J.S. *Utilitarianism, Ethical Theories,* ed. A.I. Melden, Prentice-Hall, 1967.

Moore, G.E. *Principia Ethica,* Cambridge University Press, 1976.

Moravia, Alberto. *The Red Book and The Great Wall,* Pelican, 1968.

Morgenthau, Hans. In Peter Falk, *Law, Morality and War in The Contemporary World,* Greenwood, 1984.

Muggeridge, Malcolm. *The Thirties,* Fontana Books, 1971.

Nagel, Thomas. "Ruthlessness in Public Life," *Public and Private Morality,* Cambridge University Press, 1978.

Nye, Joseph. *Nuclear Ethics,* The Free Press, 1986.

Plato. *The Republic,* in *Utilitarianism, Ethical Theories,* ed. A. I. Melden, Prentice-Hall, 1967.

Quine, J.V.W. "Two Dogmas of Empiricism," *From a Logical Point of View,* Harper Torchbooks, 1963.

———— "On the Nature of Moral Values," *Theories and Things,* Harvard University Press, 1981.

Rawls, John. *A Theory of Justice,* Oxford University Press, 1973.

Rousseau, Jean-Jacques. *Confessions,* Penguin Classics, London, 1953.

Russell, Bertrand. *A History of Western Philosophy,* Allen and Unwin, 1961.

Santayana, George. "Americanism," *Santayana on America,* Harcourt, Brace and World, 1968.

Sidgewick, Henry. *The Methods of Ethics, Ethical Theories,* ed. A.I. Melden, Prentice-Hall, 1967.

Spengler, Oswald. *The Decline of the West,* Random House, 1932.

de Tocqueville, Alexis. *Democracy in America,* The New American Library, 1956.

Webb, Beatrice. *My Apprenticeship,* Penguin Modern Classics, 1971.

Webb, Beatrice and Sidney. *Soviet Communism: A New Civilization,* Gollanz Left Book Club, 1937.

Wells, H.G. *The New Machiavelli,* Odhams Press, London.

Yeats, W.B. *Collected Poems of W.B. Yeats,* Macmillan, 1979.